The Naked Neuroscientist

By

Oliver Baggs

One Man's Unlikely Climb up the Academic Ladder

and the Lessons Learned along the Way

"Don't be interesting – be interested"

– my motto

**"Be equally grateful for what happens
and what does <u>not</u> happen"**

– another motto of mine

"Don't bite my finger, look where I am pointing!"

– attributed to Warren McCulloch

Foreword

Spoiler alert: I'm not Oliver Baggs, much less Oliver Sacks. The pen name is my way of attempting to keep this memoir honest and yet quasi-discreet, coming as it does from the pen of Neil R. Smalheiser. In this book, I describe many of the experiences that have influenced my philosophy of doing scientific research in an academic setting. This is neither an autobiography nor a retrospective of my scientific career, but rather focuses on lessons that I have learned over the years. And no naked romps, but I do plan to bare my soul.

My decision to write this book was influenced by several recent events. One was a dinner with a colleague who has been an assistant professor in a linguistics department, voicing frustration with the fact that his computational interests don't really fit in well with the more traditional, theoretically oriented faculty. Could I give him advice? Certainly not, but I could try to show him how I had handled similar situations. Through the miracle of Facebook, I had recently ordered three memoirs authored or edited by FB friends: "Trains", by Kim Dallesandro, tells of the time she was kidnapped by the Red Army faction as a teenager in 1968 Germany. "Bound", by Elizabeth Anne Wood, describes how the author took care of her terminally ill mother, the twist being that the mother had started a late-life career as a dominatrix. "The Shepherd and the Nymph", edited by David Steinberg, is a collection of a couple's raw, honest, erotic letters written in 1980s New York. All three are extremely specific, personal, snapshots into unique circumstances, with no simple take-home messages to offer, and yet I think I understood why they were written and why so many readers would find them compelling and thought-provoking.

I should also add the vivid "Kitchen Confidential" by Anthony Bourdain to this list as well, though (full disclosure) he was not my Facebook friend. Even more closely related to my memoir is "How to Fail at almost Everything and still Win Big" by Scott Adams, since I do a lot of failing, and since his discussion of pursuing process vs. pursuing goals is exemplary, even though I would not add Scott Adams as Facebook friend even if I could.

These memoirs also offered a personal antidote to the scientific memoir genre which has generated numerous classics – such as "Advice to a Young Investigator" by Ramon y Cajal, and "Honest Jim", excuse me, "The Double Helix", by James Watson. I have used these books myself in my classes, and feel they are very valuable contributions that every young scientist should read. And yet, I have no interest in writing another book of this type. Once an author has won the Nobel Prize, I feel they lose all credibility, not only prospectively, but retrospectively as well! Why, you ask? Readers will assume that their rise to stardom was inevitable, and will read their advice as if they knew what they were doing all along, or as if their success can be replicated by following in their footsteps.

As it is, I have experienced a lot of interesting twists and turns during the course of my career, having been declared moribund at least three times, only finally to become not only tenured but a full professor at a major university. I run my own lab, carry out personally fulfilling research on my own terms, and have managed to avoid more than a token amount of administrative and teaching responsibilities. Best of all, I can go anywhere without being mobbed, since I have avoided the pitfalls of fame and prizes.

I think the experiences and lessons that I absorbed are worth telling. Some should be taken as a warning, some as an exemplar, yet the stories are ambiguous because the same character flaws that have caused my crashes have also been the source of my successes. Hopefully this book will be read by my sons, and perhaps by a few of my Facebook friends as well. And if some budding investigator picks it up to bounce ideas off of, that would be cool too.

Finally, remember that this is a book of stories. Although I have tried to be accurate, these are my subjective recollections and I have emphasized the lessons learned. As Warren McCulloch used to say: "Don't bite my finger, look where I am pointing!" I plan to keep footnotes and references to a minimum, but an objective and reasonably comprehensive record of my academic curriculum vitae is included in the Appendix, for those who would like to keep track.

TABLE OF CONTENTS

Chapter One. Growing up in eastern Iowa

Backyard Scientist

I was born in Manhattan to Jewish parents, both native New Yorkers. My father had just spent 10 years working as a psychologist for Smiley Blanton and Norman Vincent Peale while going to graduate school at night. As soon as he got his PhD, he wanted to get as far away from New York as possible, and headed to the far corner of civilization, in Mount Pleasant, Iowa, testing inmates at the Iowa Psychiatric Hospital. I was 3 years old, and remained in relatively small towns all my childhood– Burlington, Davenport, and Bettendorf, where my father designed a suburban house/office, and where I attended junior high and high school.

My early memories of Burlington are vague. I remember that my third grade teacher met with my parents and asked them not to give me books to read, because I was reading way ahead of grade level and they could not keep up with me. In Davenport, I used to lay down in the backyard looking at the bugs and worms. I planted carrots and pulled them up prematurely to see how the roots were doing. I played with chemistry sets. I followed stars with star charts, and the biggest present of my entire childhood was a reflector telescope, which I used for years and eventually donated to the high school science department.

I made one original scientific discovery as a kid, namely, I noticed that putting transparent plastic objects in front of polarized light made the light rotate. I wrote this up in a paper and when I was through, I happened to see the entry "Optical Activity" in the dictionary and realized that this was already a well known phenomenon. I cited the dictionary entry in my paper, which I believe was demonstrated as a science fair project.

High School

Altogether I started school a year early, skipped two grades, and during junior high was commuted to the high school to take math classes. So I was precocious. Nevertheless, even though I spoke like a professor even then, I thought I had a pretty normal high school experience. I wrestled on the freshman team, got a varsity letter in track, and played French horn in the band. I even tried out for the tennis team, but unlike my elder brother David, who was first string, I was so bad they told me to practice a mile away from the school, on a court at a monastery, without any coaches present. They told me I was on the team but I had my doubts.

It was the late 1960s, but although we were all Beatles fanatics and played the latest vinyls as soon as they came out, the counterculture had not hit Bettendorf yet. I did meet a nice Jewish girl who had been to San Francisco and had seen hippies having sex in hallways in Haight-Ashbury. I lost my virginity to her (I was 15, she 18), but otherwise missed the 60s entirely.

I remember taking an aptitude test which was actually pretty sophisticated, since it took into account both the number as well as the specific kind of interests. The results were in: I should be a librarian! For a budding scientist/physician this seemed as far from the truth as if it said I should be a whaler. However, I must admit that forty years later, my work in information and data science does come amusingly close to librarianship.

My most memorable teacher in high school was a young, eccentric English teacher. (Was it Mr. Mund? Mr. Moore? There is a poet, Gary Moore, who resembles him and his poetry resembles my teacher's, though I can't verify that they are the same person.) I definitely remember that his name was Gary because he became engaged to another teacher, Diana, and the students would taunt them by singing a slightly modified version of the song from Music Man: "Gary in Diana, Gary in Diana, Gary in Diana"! One day he played two pieces of classical music and asked the students to compare and contrast the different personalities of the composers as reflected in their music. As it happened, we did not have a lot of classical music at home, but we did have both of the pieces he played so I was onto him (both were by Beethoven, so it was a trick assignment).

The norm in Bettendorf was to marry your high school sweetheart right after graduation and go work at a factory. I left high school after 3 years and completed my credits in the summer so I could move on to the University of Iowa. I had also qualified for full tuition to anywhere since I was a National Merit Finalist (not semi-finalist, thank you), but noticed that there was a lot of fine print around that. My parents felt I was too young (at 16) to go too far from home, plus, tuition was only $500 per semester at U of Iowa, so there was no question about where I would go. As it was, I got a full tuition scholarship to the Honors program there, so only needed to earn money for room and board.

Fuller Brush man

Selling Fuller Brush door to door not only paid my way through college, but taught me how to be a salesman – a skill that everyone should learn, regardless of what you do in life. Fuller Brush would hire literally anyone who applied, but they needed to make quota in order to keep selling, and new people were often given the worst routes. Students from the nearby Palmer College of Chiropractic liked to be Fuller Brush salesmen since they tended to be immigrants and already had the self-made mentality that it takes to sell successfully.

For some reason that I never fully understood, we were not given licenses to sell (probably cost too much) and I never thought about getting a license for myself (probably was too young at 16 and 17), so we were scofflaws and occasionally were picked up by the police, though we were released after they contacted our distributor and he received a warning. One day I was picked up and sitting in the squad car when the dispatch sent my squad car to investigate a person slumped over the wheel of a car in the neighborhood. I was amused to find that it was my brother David, who was taking a nap while the rest of us were working!

The Fuller Brush spiel is simple: We knock on the door, and offer the homeowner a choice of free gift, perhaps a scrub brush or spatula. We ask them a series of structured questions designed to learn if they have any needs that we might fill – hairbrushes, cleaning products? Are they familiar with Fuller Brush already? Here are our current specials and discounts. If we cannot go through the catalog with them, at least we leave them with the catalog and our contact information. Each neighborhood has a characteristic percentage of people who place an order, and an average order size, so the more doors we knock on, the more money we will make, with some predictability. We take (say) 90% rejection in stride, and move on, because that simply means that 10% will make a purchase.

A good, experienced salesman might have double the rate of orders than a rookie, but even so, that means 80% rejection instead of 90% (or, 20% with orders instead of 10%). These lessons were taken to heart by me and have oriented my grant writing to this day. I know at least three investigators personally who got discouraged after writing only one or two proposals and left academia, giving up on a research career entirely. Clearly they should have learned the art of salesmanship in school. Regardless of how well you write, how good the ideas are, how famous you are, you might get 1/3 or maybe only 1/6 of your proposals funded. And that is just no different from selling cars, or yachts, or indeed Fuller Brush door to door. Besides playing percentages, I learned to see things from the buyer's point of view, not just my own; to offer a free gift (in grant writing that is referred to as Preliminary Studies!); and to ask the right questions in the right order, at the right time.

In fact, the theme of Asking Questions is, in my mind, central not only to being a salesman. Being a scientist too is the art of asking the right questions, and then following up by asking more questions in a structured manner. Graduate school stresses learning methods, designing experiments, and running controls, but they do not emphasize enough that you need to begin with a good question in the first place. Once a person comes up with a hypothesis or possible answer/explanation, they tend to become attached to it and lose objectivity. But people do not become attached to questions, and thinking of experimental design as a series of structured questions will avoid the subjectivity problem.

I will go even further and say that in my mind, the definition of an intelligent person is someone who asks a lot of questions. True, that is also the definition of an interested person, since someone un-interested will not bother to probe with any questions at all. When I meet someone, whether professionally or socially, I pay close attention to what and how many questions they ask, and that is probably the most important single thing that I process. I don't really trust the words -- the content of what people say to me -- since that may reflect social niceties or the attempt to make an impression. But I can tell whether they ask questions or not, and that forms a large part of my intuition, ultimately, thanks to my Fuller Brush experience.

Visiting the Field Museum

Growing up in Iowa, we took an annual family drive to Chicago and always attended a Cubs game. Usually we visited one of the major museums, either the Museum of Science and Industry or the Field Museum. (Strangely, I don't remember going to the Art Institute back then.) We loved MSI as all kids do, but my favorite part of the Field Museum wasn't the stuffed animal exhibits, the dinosaurs, or the cavemen habitats. Rather, I loved to look at the monographs in the gift shop! This was when gift shops were not just selling trinkets to tourists, but actually carried scientific literature. I remember Karl P. Schmidt had written a series of monographs on frogs and amphibians of various locales, both local and exotic, published by the Field Museum on its own imprint, *Fieldiana*. Monographs were exciting and inspirational to me because they conveyed adventure and knowledge for its own sake. How many people do you think have read "A new turtle from the Paleocene of Colorado"? One also thinks of Gregor Mendel, whose monographs on inheritance in peas was one of the great breakthroughs in genetics, yet un-noticed by the scientific establishment for decades. I looked up Karl Schmidt and found out that he was not only Curator at the Field Museum, but had been elected to the National Academy of Sciences, a very high honor and rare for a descriptive naturalist. And more: When Marlin Perkins sent him a snake to examine, which bit him, he did not take its bite seriously at first, but then proceeded to document the physiological effects of this bite upon his body as it slowly killed him. This was his final scientific paper, published posthumously.

My love of monographs started with Schmidt, and is one of the reasons that I have decided to write this book! Interestingly, after retiring to Israel, my father wrote and self-published a monograph on Day of Remembrance postage, envelopes, and condolence letters issued each year by the Ministry of Defense to families of fallen soldiers. After his death, the Society of Israel Philatelists updated his book and published a second edition, in view of its value. You might not be able to imagine a more arcane, specialized type of information, and yet it found a lasting niche and was greatly appreciated.

Hitchhiking to class

During the summer between my first and second year at U of Iowa, I took a summer class in Linear Algebra but was living at home. To get to class twice a week, I would hitchhike from Bettendorf to Iowa City and back, about an hour each way to drive and, of course, somewhat longer when thumbing a ride. This was as stupid an idea as it sounds, but it actually worked well until one day when on I-80, a driver stopped and I declined to get in because I did not like his looks. Immediately, the next car stopped and asked me why I had not taken that ride. I explained that I was being cautious, and then got in with them.

They were two thirty-ish guys, unshaven, wearing Hawaiian shirts. I believe that they were drinking cans of beer, and had a strong Vegas vibe. One of them asked me, "I bet you got a pretty good buzz on, don't you?" I acted like I did not understand, and the other one said, "No he ain't." I got the strong impression that they were on the lam from Vegas, possibly having robbed someplace or someone. After about a half hour, they stopped for gas, and when they opened the trunk, I saw a box of diapers and fishing tackle, suggesting the car was stolen too. So I needed to make a split decision: Get back in the car again like nothing is wrong? If I do, I am taking a big risk. If I don't, they will surely know that I figured out their game, and might be in even bigger danger. I got back in the car with them until we reached Bettendorf, and they let me out.

What I learned from this experience, besides never to hitchhike again, is the power of playing stupid in the face of adversity. Little did I realize how often I would resort to this strategy during my professional career!

Chapter Two. College days

Chug, chug, chug!!! No, this is not a chapter about the fun times on campus, although I did see Led Zeppelin, Elton John, and Commander Cody when they were new on the scene. I thought that U of Iowa was a stellar academic environment, and I thrived there. In terms of lessons learned about doing science? I can think of a few episodes....

As an entering freshman, all of us had to meet with our assigned academic advisor to plan out our college scenario. I told mine that I planned to graduate in 3 years with a double major in math and premed. He told me that I was dreaming and should find something realistic. Lesson learned? Advisors are not actually giving *you* advice, since they don't actually know you and your abilities. Instead, they are giving some generic spiel to some generic student. Fortunately, I did not listen to him and proceeded to graduate in 3 years with a double major in math and Zoology (premed) with Honors.

I originally planned to be a physics major, but found that I did not like anyone in my intro physics class! After I switched to major in math, I learned that all of the folks I had disliked in that class were not physics majors either. Speaking of math, I am no prodigy whatsoever and yet I enjoyed both the theoretical and practical aspects of math. This was in the early days of computers (I had programmed using punch tape and punch cards), when both computer science and statistics were part of the math department. I still refer to my college math and statistics textbooks, and the clear, logical explanations I received as an undergrad have held me in good stead for the next 40+ years. One of the few pieces of advice that I will give unsolicited is: Take as much math as you can stand, you will never regret it. (Bear in mind the paragraph above which says don't take generic advice.)

My first neurobiology course was with Rodney K. Murphey, then a first-year faculty member just starting his lab, later to become a program officer at NSF and a champion of studying invertebrate nervous systems. In his final exam, one of the questions that Rod asked students was to imagine a brain without action potentials. How would a brain without action potentials necessarily differ from one with action potentials? Action potentials are electric spikes that travel down the axons of neurons. Without action potentials, the axons can't be very long, hence the body must be very small. Also, action potentials are triggered at a certain threshold in an all-or-none fashion, so the frequency of action potentials conveys most of the information from one neuron to another, in contrast to graded electrical changes which would influence one neuron to another without action potentials. Many invertebrates lack neurons with action potentials, whereas most vertebrates have them.

This simple question blew my mind for two separate reasons. First, here was a final exam which did not ask the student to regurgitate facts, but instead demanded that the student think both logically and creatively. I have tried to keep up that philosophy in my own teaching. Second, he encouraged the students to glimpse not just actual brains, but to imagine POSSIBLE brains, even those that might not exist in nature. This was a life-changing moment which underpinned my much later studies of literature-based discovery – a type of analysis which identifies surprising ideas and hypotheses that are not necessarily likely to be true, but whose virtues suggest that they are worth studying and testing further.

I asked Rod if I could do a laboratory project with him, and he suggested that I try to identify the nerves that convey the sensation of touch in the leg of the cricket. I spent months trying to unsuccessfully build a solenoid magnet which would reversibly lift a piece of metal a few inches, thus creating a gentle, reproducible tap on the table. In retrospect, I should have just tapped the table myself with my finger! Also, when I cut one nerve, it moved the rest of the ganglia and because the tension became altered, and this affected the pattern of action potentials traveling down the remaining nerves. I never did solve this problem (which would have taken Rod about a half hour to do). Somehow, I was not the slightest bit discouraged by this obvious incompetence and evident lack of talent for working with my hands. Nor did it sway me against doing electrophysiologic studies as a graduate student later. However, when I became a faculty member, every time I am approached by a student who wants to do a rotation "to see if I like science", I caution them that their experience in any single lab is really a crapshoot. Someone who likes working with electrodes might not like working with test tubes or with mice. A scientist should not choose projects because they like the techniques involved, indeed, as they move from project to project, the techniques are likely to change as well.

Louis Pasteur is an extreme example of this: He started out trying to learn why beer was spoiling in a brewery (industrial applied question), identified that chemical compounds associated with fermentation had different crystal structures than those not associated (geology); studied the basis of fermentation and debunked spontaneous generation of life (biology); and eventually devised a rabies vaccine (medicine).

My undergraduate Honors thesis was not based on my work with Rod, but was an independent study course in which I reviewed what was known about the brain structures involved in vision. The relevant aspect of this is that I only read primary research articles -- no review articles or books -- and synthesized the ideas myself. Actually, this was not because I wanted to be intellectually independent – I just was unaware that review articles were available! However, it taught me how to handle the scientific literature efficiently, and was the first of many, many times that I have performed syntheses of scientific topics.

My course in developmental biology was with David Soll, another new faculty member who was later to become internationally prominent. I have to compare David Soll with Frank Zappa, both in appearance and in personality. He was married to a ballet dancer who lived on the east coast (evidently an open marriage), and was dating one of the graduate students in the department. He used to give me notes to pass to her.

His final exam was a take-home question: "There is a lot of RNA residing in the nucleus which does not code for any protein. How can one design an experiment to test what this RNA does?" As I ruminated on this question, I went through the stacks of the library, opening bound journal volumes at random. Believe it or not, I ran across an article by Richard Firtel in a journal called *Experientia*, which outlined an approach to this very question in the slime mold! As it happened, this was an outstanding research question, not something hypothetical, and I had stumbled onto the solution by chance.

In retrospect, I tie this experience with the informatics concept called "undiscovered public knowledge", which refers to knowledge that is public (i.e. present in publications) yet which no one knows, because no one has read it -- either because the text is hard to find, or because the information resides in more than one document and one needs to put together the pieces to form a whole.

Chapter Three. Interviewing for medical school

As graduation approached, I began interviewing for medical schools. I was not constrained to attend U of Iowa anymore, so I applied to a half-dozen places. As it happened, U of Iowa had a policy wherein any Iowa resident who attended U of Iowa, took the prerequisites and had a good-enough grade point average, was automatically accepted without requiring an interview. Unfortunately, Iowa did not offer a MD-PhD program, and if I tried to do MD and PhD in tandem there, I would not qualify for scholarships in either program. In contrast, there were a handful of integrated MD-PhD programs and I targeted those. During this process, I learned something very important about myself – I am a terrible interviewee!

At Harvard (I believe this was the Harvard-MIT joint program), they asked me some softball question and my reply indicated that I was skeptical of the germ theory of disease! What I was referring to was simply the "seed and soil" hypothesis, articulated well by Paget, in which both a germ and a susceptible state of the host were required for a disease to take hold. But the interviewer took me to be a blithering idiot and the interview was short.

At another school, the interviewer asked me who my favorite author was. Again, a softball question. I said "Edgar Allan Poe" and he said "I HATE Edgar Allan Poe." This was not a stress interview – he did not want to see how I would handle his response – rather, he was saying that anyone who liked Poe must be a madman or degenerate, and again, the interview was short.

I recognized that my blundering in interviews was something that I must conquer. I never did so. I have managed to avoid being interviewed almost entirely for the rest of my life, but on the rare occasions when I have been interviewed (e.g., years later, by headhunters looking for potential administrators), I still blow it big time.

Inexplicably, my interview for Albert Einstein College of Medicine went well. They allowed me to interview with an alumnus living near Chicago, rather than having to fly to New York, and I met the surgeon Sidney Levitsky at his office at UIC (University of Illinois at Chicago). I arrived in the Chicago loop in the morning, and since the interview was not until the afternoon, I ate lunch at Tad's Steak House and watched John Wayne in True Grit, before taking the El to UIC. Note that I can remember this trip in much greater detail than the others, including the name of my interviewer! Yet I do not remember any particular questions or answers, other than that he seemed to regard me as a peer.

I was actually not admitted to the regular MD program, but rather directly to the MD-PhD program headed by Steve Baum, which was nice because I was given full tuition and a stipend for a 6 year accelerated program. Steve Baum had a refreshing attitude: He was not looking for good students who would get straight As – rather, he wanted to identify people who would cure cancer someday. Not sure that anyone in my class found "the cure for cancer", but we certainly comprised an eccentric lot of over-achievers, as I found out when I moved to the East Bronx and entered a dorm on campus, located in the middle of an Italian residential neighborhood.

Chapter Four. New York years 1974-1982

There were seven of us entering the MD-PhD program, of whom I especially remember Josh Zimmerberg, Ellen Weinberg, Lee Kaplan, and Donna Vogel, all of whom went on to have interesting and productive careers. Actually, many if not most of my other classmates went on to have interesting and productive careers too – off the top of my head, Sten Vermund and his soulmate Pilar Vargas-Lizardi, Steven Snyder, Moshe Levi, Myles Akabas, Stanley Schein, Schlomo Shinnar, etc.

My primary partners in crime, during the preclinical classroom years, were my classmates Charlie Mick and David Rosenbaum. Most of our stories cannot be repeated here…. Okay, just one. We were down in the Village and ordered a pitcher of beer. As we sat and drank, and as the pitcher was almost empty, we noticed that there was vomit floating in the pitcher. We brought this to the attention of the barkeep, who shrugged and said, "You drank it, didn't cha?"

You might think that a kid who grew up in small towns in Iowa would have difficulty adapting to New York City. But I embraced the entire city, both scientifically and otherwise. Remember, though, that I was a poor student, still teenaged, which kept me blissfully out of trouble. I missed Studio 54, AIDS, Plato's Retreat, the Playboy Mansion, even nice restaurants like Tavern on the Green. Instead, I made many trips to Anthology Film Archives in Soho, where Jonas Mekas screened experimental films; to Famous Ray's pizza on 6th

Avenue (best pizza in the entire world, defines New York style perfectly; they add mushrooms or other ingredients to precooked pizza, cover again with cheese, and bake again until the cheese is bubbling); and to Chinatown for cheap pork chop noodle soup at a place that was open 24 hours.

Soon after arriving at Einstein, one of the older students asked us freshmen if we were interested in listening to free jazz down in the Village. We all said "Sure!!" but when we arrived (via subway train from the Bronx), we found that the jazz was free but the cover charge wasn't. I lent one of the other students the money to enter and felt like a rich sugar daddy. I did see a few other jazz greats during my time in New York, notably Pharoah Sanders, but missed the chance to hear Zoot Sims because I thought the name Zoot was silly. Still kicking myself for that one.

Brushes with fame

I am a walker and spent endless hours walking in Manhattan, both North-South and East-West. Once I walked from Battery Park in the south all the way up to the Cloisters.

One evening, while walking uptown on Sixth Avenue, I saw a limo stop in front of a pizza parlor and a man waited to pick up several large boxes of pizza. As I kept walking further uptown, about twenty minutes later, the limo stopped in front of a strip club and three strippers came out and entered the limo. I saw Rod Stewart in the back seat.

Another time, I saw Andy Warhol three different times in the course of twenty-four hours. The first was at the Plaza Hotel on the West Side, where I was having lunch with my uncle Lawrence. He wanted me to invest my (nonexistent) savings with him, but I told him he should put money in a new business venture called Genentech, just getting underway. (Factoid: Genentech became the first biotechnology firm and a fantastic success.) Andy was at the next table, sitting with several guys in suits. Later that night, I was at the Mudd Club in lower Manhattan and he was there with John Cale and Nico. The next morning, I saw him walking two little dogs near his place in Gramercy Park on the East Side. I think the meaning of these chance encounters is obvious. Of the visits to CBGB and Mudd Club, the most memorable (a rare outing which my future wife Sue attended with me) was Mande Dahl, a singer who seemed to be deliberately bad, and ended her act by flashing one of her boobs. I don't remember any of the famous groups who played there, though!

A more portentous chance encounter happened during one of my walks. I happened to be crossing the street at 5th Avenue and 14th Street during a lightning storm (no rain) and saw three different lightning strikes occur almost at once. At first, the lights went out everywhere below 14th street to the left of me, and then below 14th street to the right of me, then above 14th street. Manhattan has three different circuits that power the city, and the lightning managed to knock out all three, creating the Great Blackout of 1977. I happened to be standing at the epicenter of this at the exact moment it happened. Definitely a mystical experience.

It is not entirely true that I missed all of the iconic haunts of New York. The Chelsea Hotel was famous for its musicians, artists and bohemians. Leonard Cohen wrote "Chelsea Hotel" about receiving oral sex from Janice Joplin there. Sid killed Nancy Vicious there too. I took a wine tasting course with a lady who lived at the Chelsea Hotel. She was in her 80s; holding a class allowed her to buy and taste the good stuff that otherwise she could not afford. I tasted the best Burgundies and Bordeaux of my life. I also stayed at the Chelsea Hotel overnight once: a gal of my acquaintance had her flight to Israel delayed by twelve hours, so we checked in at midnight for what turned out to be a one night stand.

Actually, this gal's story is relevant to the theme of the book. She had applied to UCLA Medical School and had received a rejection letter. Being the type of person who does not take "No" for an answer, she insisted to learn the reason and was told her grade point average was not interpretable. (See, she went to University in Israel where she had a perfect score but the Israeli grading system was not directly comparable to the US 4.0 system.) Eventually, the dean of her University had to get together with the dean of UCLA and convert her GPA to the American system. Then, she got another rejection letter, and after inquiring further, was told that this was a "clerical error". Finally she got on the waiting list, and eventually was admitted to UCLA.

One lesson from this is that polite persistence pays off. It ain't over until it's over, and even then, it ain't over. Another is to realize that decisions made by committees are not necessarily careful, logical, and wise – sometimes the rejection letter comes because a secretary picked up the wrong pile of applications!

Living at and near the Einstein campus

Albert Einstein College of Medicine is located on Morris Park Avenue right by Eastchester Road, in the East Bronx, embedded within a middle class Italian residential neighborhood. Two blocks away were Italian delis and I often had calzones or prosciutto/provolone sandwiches for lunch. Further away was a family restaurant where once a week I would get linguini with red clam sauce, a special treat.

There was a Mafioso bar situated immediately next to Einstein, the Tenda Trap, which had Cadillacs and limos double-parked outside. I was brave enough to go inside once to see it and they charged me $7 for a 7 ounce bottle of beer (a lot back then!), clearly not wanting to see my kind in there again. Much more friendly was a bar about two blocks on the other side of Eastchester Road, which had a stable of middle-aged, nicely dressed matronly women sitting at the bar. Apparently they were hookers, but they were genuinely cordial and chatty.

Walking in the neighborhood at night was dangerous, not because of street crime, but because of local Italian vigilantes who drove around carrying bats, asking everyone on the street who they were and whether they belonged there. Bear in mind that we were only a half mile from the South Bronx with an unbelievable crime rate, so I empathized with them although I did not like being stopped and questioned.

A mile northwest of Einstein was a small Jewish neighborhood, where I moved for a year. I lived downstairs from a young Orthodox Jewish couple, but when the wife kept inviting me to visit upstairs during the day when her husband was out working, I left in haste. I found an apartment just a block from the Einstein campus, shared with David Schessel, another student whose passions were orchid and giant lizards, both of whom had their own rooms within our apartment. My landlady, Mrs. Puleo, was an earthy Sicilian reminiscent of Shelly Winters, whose boyfriend was reminiscent of Anthony Quinn and who fortunately had a laisse-faire approach to the apartment.

Taking preclinical classes at Einstein

Einstein was founded only in the 1950s, after the Second World War, as a Jewish-affiliated institution. The Einstein faculty included not only former Jewish refugees but others who would not be welcome at the more established medical schools, such as Alex Novikoff, a blacklisted Communist who was a leading contender for the Nobel Prize, and Frank Lilly, the first openly gay scientist elected to the National Academy of Sciences.

My favorite quirky faculty member was probably Jacques Padawer, a full professor known as an expert on Mast cells and refiner of Nomarski microscopy, because he dressed so shabbily, with a huge ring of keys hanging from his pocket, that one could only take him for the janitor. In fact, his leadership in fashion has had a long lasting influence on me, as I have felt free to wear t-shirts and jeans to work to this day. My office in UIC is next to the IT department, and visitors tend to mistake me for a computer programmer or student intern. Each time that happens, I think of ol' Jacques Padawer and a smile comes to my lips.

I really only remember two classes that I took during the core medical curriculum: Neuroscience, organized by Dominick Purpura, and Immunology, organized by Frank Lilly. Not coincidentally, they were the only two which were essentially graduate courses with a research focus -- truly inspirational in scope and quality -- and they were the only two in which I earned a grade of Honors. The Neuroscience professors team-teaching the course were a Who's Who including Michael Bennett, Kimi Suzuki, Cedric Raine, Bill Norton, and George Pappas, among others. This is the only course whose notes I have saved. An unexpected lingering influence from this course occurred years later, when George Pappas had moved to become Chairman of Anatomy and Cell Biology at UIC, and I had an adjunct appointment in his department. I asked him to write me a letter of recommendation for something or other, and in it, he mentioned that I had complained a lot in his class at Einstein!

Courses such as Physiology and Pharmacology were certainly okay, but did not stick in my mind for long; when I took a course in Renal pathophysiology I had to relearn all of the relevant physiology and pharmacology again. In fact, I used to have a recurring dream in which I am in the first day of a new clinical rotation, and I am panicked because I have forgotten everything. These were subtle indications that perhaps clinical medicine is not my forte, though at the time I still planned to combine clinical and laboratory studies.

A normal, healthy old man

In one of our classes, a psychiatrist was set to interview a normal, healthy old man so we could learn about the issues and coping strategies faced in aging. The man was ushered in, and the psychiatrist began asking him questions, but the man began to falter, his answers were hesitant and incomplete, and he finally asked to terminate the interview. As he left, the psychiatrist began lecturing to the class: The man's hesitancy indicates blah blah blah or some such – basically, he gave psychological and psychoanalytical explanations for everything that the man had said and done.

Well, I had to leave the class early because I needed to attend a class at Columbia, so I left shortly after the man did – and saw that just on the other side of the door, the man had collapsed. Two cardiologists just happened to be walking by and started CPR. One of them asked me to find a scalpel so they could do an emergency tracheotomy. I ran down the hall (this is in a medical research building, not a clinic) and came to Robert Terry's laboratory. I came in and said, "I need a scalpel" and Terry found one and handed it to me without saying a word. Unfortunately the man expired on the spot.

It would be easy to say (and I do) that the psychiatrist blew it big time, spouting psychobabble on one side of the door and not even considering the possibility that the man was dying of a heart attack. The cardiologists saw a man with a heart attack and did not even consider the possibility that he was using psychological defense mechanisms!

But to be fair, every specialty suffers from the fact that they see patients through their own lenses. The man was said to be healthy, so the expectation was that he was healthy! If you have headaches and see a neurologist, an ENT doc, a psychiatrist, or an autoimmune specialist, the workups are likely to be quite different, as they will tend to attempt to rule in or out their own spectrum of headache causes, rather than taking an overall objective view of the situation. And, once a diagnosis is made by one doctor, others will tend to fix their interpretations around that and will incorporate new information in that context. Ever since, I have been acutely aware of the importance of questioning assumptions (and periodically reassessing them), of not accepting explanations too easily or too firmly, and most of all, asking myself if the situation might look entirely different on the other side of the door.

I also think of this episode when people ask me whether it is worthwhile getting a MD-PhD degree if they only plan to do research and not see patients. You see, Robert Terry, MD, world famous and the leading force behind Alzheimer disease at the time, did not know or recognize me at all when I ran in breathlessly to get a scalpel. He was a research pathologist, perhaps the most thoughtful line of medicine that there is, and yet in a crisis his MD training oriented him towards action, not reflection. I imagine that if I ran into the laboratory of someone with a PhD degree, they would have asked, "Who are you? What's the story? Do you really need a scalpel or would some other implement work better?" PhD training teaches one how to do research but MD training teaches one to DO research – get off your butt and cure cancer, for God's sake! In other words, I see MD training much like being in the military, with a focus on mission and strategy and boot camp, and it stays with you forever, just like military training does.

Another crisis in my first few months occurred when one of my friends living in the dorm began having an acute psychotic breakdown. I am forever grateful to Andy Doyle MD, an assistant professor of neurology, who again responded without hesitation to come to the dorm and provide comfort to him. My friend was panicked, overwhelmed with hallucinations, and was trying to calm himself down by repeating Zen slogans such as "When hungry, eat; when tired, sleep", having not slept in three or four days. Eventually I visited him in the inpatient ward of Cornell's psychiatric hospital in Westchester County. They were showing a film in the patient open area, but I noticed that they were showing the reels out of order! I also noticed that I was the only one who noticed that.

Studies and visits to other schools around town

One of my defining character traits is that I am restless. Curiously restless and restlessly curious. Restlessness manifested itself scientifically too; I wanted to experience the scientific environment not simply at Einstein, but all across New York City. I took courses at Columbia and NYU and hung-out at a variety of different laboratories.

There was a Neuroscience Graduate Student group which collated seminars and other events and distributed them across universities. The head of the group was Kerry Walton, a Communist and the sister of basketball great Bill Walton (and very tall herself). She was working with Rodolfo Llinas, one of the greats who had just come from U of Iowa (where he had a building to himself way out in the countryside to avoid electrical interference!) and landed at NYU where he was rapidly building another Neuroscience research group. Had I (and he) stayed at U of Iowa I would undoubtedly have joined his group too.

One of the perks of being in the MD-PHD program is that they provided support for students to travel to conferences and to take graduate courses in other universities. I took a course in the mathematics of morphogenesis (how organisms change shape during development) given by Jerome Percus at NYU Courant Institute, partially because it was located in Manhattan and easy walking to the West Village, the East Village, Soho, and Chinatown. This was a nice course but failed to fire my interest in doing mathematical modeling for a living.

Much more provocative was a class in the Psychology of Learning which I took at Columbia on the Westside, not far from the apartment in which my parents were living when I was born. The teacher, Herb Terrace, had been a protégé of B. F. Skinner (the behaviorist) and is today probably best known as the person who failed to teach a chimpanzee to communicate via language. His original intent was to disprove Noam Chomsky's assertion that only humans can use language, but the chimp, named Nim Chimpsky, failed to deliver, and this was taken as evidence that the attempt is futile. I think if we took a human at random and tried to teach them integral calculus and failed, we wouldn't conclude that humans lack the inherent ability – but I digress. The course was very well organized and was comprehensive, covering all types of learning (habituation, sensitization, Pavlovian conditioning, discriminant conditioning, etc.) ranging from single-celled organisms to humans. My main frustration was that they kept changing the time and day of the class, and simply announced this with a sheet of paper stuck to the classroom door – so I would commute for an hour from the Bronx only to see that class had been moved, usually to some time or day that I was unavailable.

They gave a take-home final exam. I don't remember exactly what the scientific issue was -- maybe something about they were assuming that synaptic changes that accompany learning necessarily cause learning -- but I rejected their exam and wrote a long essay of my own instead. (Years later, I learned that this is something that Walter Pitts (Chapter Five) would have done, which is probably one of the reasons I had such an affinity for him.) Herb said that even if my essay had been worthy of being published in Psychological Review, it still would not have been an acceptable exam response, and gave me a "D". I told Steve Baum, my program director, the bad news; he shrugged and said, "You passed, didn't you?" I knew I had made the right choice coming to Einstein.

I occasionally hung out at Columbia's department of Biological Sciences too. Art Mercurio and David Friedlander were students and Eduardo Macagno was a young faculty member. David was writing his thesis at the time and instead of writing in longhand and paying a typist as the rest of us did, he had programmed his own word processor! By rights he should have become a billionaire since this was before any commercial word processing apps were available, but he kept the software for himself only. There is a bar where the original beats used to drink (Kerouac, Ginsburg and Burroughs were Columbia students) and I had one drink there, but I was far more impressed with a Szechuan restaurant across the street which offered my first taste of Ma Po bean curd, still a favorite of mine.

Since my thesis was going to be on development of the retino-tectal system (more on this later), I took a field trip up to New York Medical College in Valhalla, where Sansar Sharma was one of the best, yet most under-rated investigators in that field. "Skip" Hunt was a young buck protégé of Marcus Jacobson (who wrote the definitive textbook on neural development), located at Johns Hopkins, and had published a series of high-profile papers showing that the orientation of the retina could be reprogrammed up to a certain stage in development but was then fixed. Sharma and five other labs were unable to reproduce these results, but they were denounced and dismissed as "sloppy surgeons". It took Sharma and his collaborators almost a decade to publish their own studies, which appeared in a specialty journal. Meanwhile, "Skip" Hunt had revealed a drug problem (cocaine, I think) and his meteoric rise quietly, eventually, fizzled. "Skip" was the first of several high flying hot-shots that I met during my career, most of whom left academia for industry or clinics rather than for rehab, but I grew to be suspicious of the entire lot, and more appreciative for the quiet, careful investigators.

Anyway, Sansar invited me to carry out an experiment recording from the tectum of the goldfish. He told me, use 0.01 ml of paralyzing agent, but I saw him draw up 0.1 ml in the syringe so I assumed that he misspoke. What I did not see was that he pushed most of this back out! I gave the fish 0.1 ml and it died quickly as I tried to start recording. The lesson I learned here is pretty obvious. Sansar also gave me a piece of advice that I never forgot: He said that to dress for success, choose just a few items of the highest possible quality that you can afford. Unfortunately I did not follow his advice though I agree with him, in principle. Sansar also had a young technician, who was poetic, dreamy, strikingly tall and dark, Jewish but looked Egyptian. Her parents had escaped the Nazis (were they Holocaust survivors?) and fled to Brazil, where her father made a fortune manufacturing envelopes and stationary. To this day, I tell my kids that one does not need to invent brilliant tech apps or to make shrewd investments to get rich: simply make something simple that people need, like envelopes. I visited her years later, after she had married and moved to Israel; she was glad to see me but her husband less so.

I have not mentioned my PhD thesis advisor, Stan Crain, yet, but one of his postdocs, Cheryl Dreyfus, had gotten a position working with Michael Gershon in the Anatomy department at Columbia Medical School way uptown near Harlem, and I hung out up there too. In the spirit of being in the right place at the right time, I accidentally happened to be there when Gershon had both his 40th and 50th birthday surprise parties. I attended research seminars where the big honcho was Tom Jessell; you could not avoid noticing his partner Jane Dodd because she wore a big pink streak in her hair, long before I saw that fashion statement on anyone else. At the time it was punk, though colored hair streaks have survived long beyond punk and punk sensibility.

There were still other places to go to study and hang out. The New School for Social Research on Fifth Avenue was an open, friendly place. I attended a few sherry gatherings at Rockefeller University on the upper east side, very impressed by the fact that this was a PhD program that at the time did not require students to take any formal classes at all. I attended one of the James Arthur lectures at the New York Academy of Sciences. These lectures were, in my mind, the pinnacle of thoughtful discourse, ever since I had purchased the lecture by Karl Pribram, "What Makes Man Human?" at the Field Museum in Chicago. The question has stayed with me over the years, and when I founded my own journal (Chapter Nine) I published a special issue on this theme (https://j-biomed-discovery.biomedcentral.com/articles), with contributions from many eminent scientists, and was even able to convince Pribram to write a follow-up article himself, "What Makes Humanity Humane".

But none of these venues could compare to Sarah Lawrence College in Bronxville. Charlie Mick and I went up there to study in their library. At the time, the undergraduate College was an all girls' school, which seemed to be a good way to meet the opposite sex. As a group I found them to be very sad, very talented, and very rich. We became acquainted with three of them: One was a ballet dancer, heiress to a department store fortune; one was also a ballet dancer, with great ambition equaled by self-doubt and anxiety; and the third was not a student at Sarah Lawrence at all, but was studying in the library just like we were. When I looked them up recently, I learned that the first had died slowly of MS. The third had died a hero's death saving a child who had fallen on train tracks. I don't know about the second, but I would like to imagine that she had a brilliant career as a ballet dancer and is now teaching students of her own.

PhD thesis studies and research

Stan Crain was definitely a PhD (if you recall my earlier rant about MD vs. PhD training) but was a free thinker, and had an open door policy to anyone who was interested in working with him. He made his reputation working with Murray Bornstein and Edith Peterson; the latter two ran a tissue culture laboratory that cultivated pieces of nervous tissue from the developing mouse, and in their expert hands, had been able to achieve surprising levels of maturity in vitro. These so-called organotypic explants were able to extend axon bundles that became myelinated (which was used as a model for studying multiple sclerosis, among other things), and that established complex networks of spiking neurons. Stan was the electrophysiologist of the group, who not only characterized the patterns of electrical activity (used as a model of seizures, for example) but also showed that sensory ganglia placed near spinal cord extended axons that invaded the cord and made synapses that had the right placement and the right pharmacology. He used this as a model to study pain pharmacology. Late in life, after I graduated, he discovered ultra-potent opioid effects at 1,000 times lower doses than usually used clinically, and formed a start-up company to investigate this and create new pain medications that would avoid addiction potential.

Stan was balding, about six feet tall, with long white hair and a right eye that looked to the far wall. His wife, Bea, assisted him in the lab, and was as much of a flower child as a suburban mom could hope to be. This was back in the days when scientists had secretaries, and Stan's secretary was Debbie, whose gum-chewing, wise-cracking demeanor fit in well with her thick Brooklyn accent.

Although Stan had a string of postdocs including Alcmene Chalazonitis, Cheryl Dreyfus, and Manny Pollack, I was his first graduate student – if you don't count Steve Baer, who had left the program before graduating. His reputation not only preceded me, it seems he looked a lot like me – Jewish with a Jew-'fro - - and Murray Bornstein called me Steve for the full six years that I was in the group. Murray apparently made a comment about me that I acted as if I had been a P. E. major in college. At the time I assumed that he never distinguished between me and Steve Baer. The Steve Baer story that I heard was about the time that he was making a burgoo, some sort of southern stew, that needed to cook slowly on a stovetop. Then then went out and did not return for several days, having forgotten the burgoo, and found it was nothing but a solid residue – from a burgoo to a goo, as it were. I did manage to track down Steve Baer before I left New York. He was performing at the Museum of Modern Art in an outdoor courtyard, some type of ambient electronic music resembling whale sounds filtered through a digeridoo. I said hello and introduced myself. He was not impressed, probably having not heard any burgoo stories about me.

Murray Bornstein was definitely a MD, who saw patients and was an expert trial witness as well as a researcher. He was very meticulous in running the laboratory with a firm hand, since quality control is essential for tissue culture: There was a story about a period of time when the cultures stopped developing, and they could not find anything wrong -- until one day he noticed that the technician was dunking his crucifix made of copper into the nitric acid bath used to clean the glassware. Enough copper came off the crucifix to contaminate the glass and ruin the entire project.

The actual tissue culture laboratory was run by three technicians: Tara Finnigan, Rachel Sheppard, and Cass Kirk. I loved them all. Rachel was the lab supervisor for several years; I remember how much angst Tara had when she had the opportunity to be promoted to supervisor, since she would now have to tell her friends what to do. I was glad when she moved up, and eventually Tara became a lawyer in Florida. Cass was restless, like me, and actually the one who had cooked the burgoo with Steve Baer. She did not stay long because she went to the west coast to run another tissue culture laboratory, and later to Boston and beyond.

But the most lovable of all was Edith Peterson, a crusty, chain-smoking, red-faced little troll and I mean this in the sweetest and cutest way possible. Edith had the magic hands that had made all of the "firsts" of the tissue culture laboratory happen. She had never gotten a PhD degree, and her academic title was the lowest possible that would allow her to write her own grant proposals. She was funded by the Muscular Dystrophy Association for many years. Once I drove with Edith to a conference in Montreal, and noticed that she kept the same amount of pressure on the accelerator, whether we went uphill or downhill. On one of the downhills, she flew past a state trooper who was standing on the side of the road waving his arms vigorously. We worried that maybe he needed assistance, so Edith stopped and very, very, very slowly backed up about a quarter mile on the shoulder of the highway. When she finally reached him, he gave her a speeding ticket! I met her husband only once or twice briefly – he was apparently disabled and did not leave their Bronx apartment very often. When Edith retired, Einstein did the unthinkable – they gave her an Honorary degree in a big ceremony, standing next to the philanthropist Mary Lasker and a U.S. senator. I cannot imagine another institution recognizing pure unheralded scientific scholarship and accomplishment as exemplified by Edith.

Just like "Alice's Restaurant" eventually has to talk about Alice, so should I mention what I did for my PhD thesis studies. Whereas Stan and Edith had shown that sensory ganglia could form appropriate synaptic connections in the spinal cord, sensory ganglia are part of the peripheral nervous system. I created cultures of retina, which is part of the central nervous system, and showed that in culture they could develop normally, form optic nerves, and respond to light. When placed near pieces of superior colliculus (a.k.a. the tectum, one of its normal targets) the optic nerves could invade and form connections with it, but did not do so with the spinal cord (not a natural target). Moreover, there was an appropriate mapping of the projections where one part of the retina formed connections with the correct part of the superior colliculus. Altogether this work, which demonstrated a high degree of neural specificity in culture (i.e. lacking the other cues present in the intact embryo), resulted in six publications. As well, I developed a theoretical model which took several years to ripen but eventually was published as well, making a total of seven for my graduate period, which was not too shabby. I was quite proud of this body of investigations.

Ritchie Simson and "Standard Deviations"

It would have been too easy, and not "me", to focus single-mindedly on my PhD studies. I wanted to balance this with doing something entirely different, and moreover something in which I was a fish out of water with no talent or inclinations whatsoever. This may be the best example of my personality quirk which you can view as a constant challenge to shake up the brain, or just a perverse streak.

Regardless, I joined a technician in the department, Richard (Ritchie) Simson, in writing a Broadway-style musical comedy! Ritchie was an enthusiastic attendee at the BMI Musical Theatre Workshop. I had no ear for writing music, which he handled solely, but we spent many hours brainstorming and writing the book and lyrics, which of course was on the theme of academic medicine, and of course was called "Standard Deviations". Altogether I think we worked on this for three years. At one point, Ritchie was illegally subletting a nice apartment on the West Side in the same building as Darren McGavin, who rode up the elevator with us once.

As for our play's style, think of "A Funny Thing Happened on the Way to the Forum". The villain is the chairman of the department, a neurosurgeon named Rupert Ripmov. The hero is Gabe Lingam, student of idealistic researcher Warren Goodrich. Gabe is enamored with Warren's technician Rita. Gabe's mother, the earthy Betty Rorschach-Lingam, provides extra comic relief, as does the government auditor Ms. Prigh who is investigating Ripmov's books. The lyrics were chock-full of priceless gems, for example, "Love is a boat two people row" and "Our furry friends must give us pause / our furry friends must give us paws".

Our script and demo tape were rejected by the top people on Broadway -- not to name-drop but Howard Ashman personally read and rejected us. Nevertheless, this project was a resounding success: Ritchie was friends with a guy who was room-mates with the actor John Phillips (known professionally as Ethan Phillips, a.k.a. Neelix on Star Trek: Voyager). In turn, John was friends with Michael Seidman, a nephrologist who was engaged to Ellen, whose best friend was Susan Greene. Ritchie invited me, they invited them, and we all converged in

Phillips' Manhattan loft for a New Year's Eve party at the turn of 1978. When they played Auld Lang Syne, I kissed Sue, and we started dating, eventually to marry (for 39 years and counting).

"Standard Deviations" was a success more directly too. We did rent a theatre and held a staged reading with actors that we had auditioned and rehearsed. Sue sold iced tea and snacks. Interestingly, I found a discarded script in the theatre and began first reading it, then laughing. Turns out it was a scene from "Torch Song Trilogy" and Harvey Fierstein had just held the staged reading there before us.

My carefree Broadway days happened not long before AIDS hit New York. Ritchie's roommate succumbed as did Howard Ashman, Keith Haring and so many others. Ritchie did not ever launch a musical production on his own, but he eventually took over the BMI Musical Theatre workshop and has continued to inspire budding writers for many years. My collaboration with Ritchie presaged a similar "garage band" collaboration that I was to pursue with Don Swanson later.

One final thing that persists from these Einstein days: Sue still calls me Steve when we both need a laugh.

7th year: Clinical rotations

I survived my required rotations in Jacobi Hospital, a large municipal hospital in the Bronx where I did medicine; the small Einstein hospital where I did OB-

GYN; and Montefiore Hospital, the private hospital in the North Bronx where I did surgery (and where Sue was working as a registered nurse, so that we actually worked together for a brief spell). I even went to St. Barnabas Hospital, a chronic care hospital famous for having Oliver Sacks on staff, and I did a series of psychiatry classes at a hospital in the heart of the South Bronx.

I remember a homeless man, a decrepit geezer, who came in to Jacobi with advanced gangrene in his leg. The residents told him quite frankly that he needed to have an emergency amputation to save his life, and he resolutely refused to give permission. He stayed in bed a week, then another week, then another. The infection walled itself off, was eventually resolved on IV antibiotics, and he walked out of the hospital – on two legs.

In contrast, a healthy, middle-aged man appeared in Montefiore for an elective hernia repair. I say hernia but it was the size of a basketball, maybe the size of two basketballs. It did not bother him, but his doctors thought it would be a good idea to get it fixed. The night after surgery, he had a pulmonary embolus and died.

If you ask why I am loathe to recommend surgery of any kind, I am probably thinking of these two patients from my student days.

On the other hand, I also had a patient who needed surgery (maybe it was a gunshot wound) but the resident was very reluctant to send him at night, because the success rate was very low for the night shift in a municipal hospital. He temporized by restricting fluids, which was a mistake as the attending pointed out the next morning. He should have pushed fluids instead. The patient never got the chance to go into surgery, but went into shock instead and died.

On the lighter side, during my rotation in psychiatry I attended a lecture but I was literally running late and when I got to class, my feet were boiling. I took off my shoes in the classroom, and the psychiatrist, Dr. Charles Socarides, scowled: "Don't take off your shoes. I am not a homosexual!" I looked him up later and found that he was a major opponent of removing homosexuality as a mental disorder in the DSM (which had occurred in 1973, just a few years earlier). Seems he had homosexuality on his mind too much, if you ask me.

Okay, back to real life in the South Bronx. I followed a child psychiatrist as he interviewed an 8 year old boy who had suddenly become depressed. His patient, insightful questioning allowed this little boy to be able to reveal that he had seen his classmate pushed to his death from a window in the public projects where they lived. The interview only took twenty minutes or so, did not attempt to deal with anything psychoanalytical or biochemical, yet changed that little boy's life and mine.

Since I mentioned Oliver Sacks in this section, this might be a good place to mention that City Island is a sleepy, bohemian enclave not far from Einstein -- in fact, it is within easy biking distance -- yet it is a world away. Visiting City Island, you can imagine how Key West must have been in the days of Hemingway. Oliver Sacks famously lived there, though I never met him (nor anywhere during his life). Suzanne Zukin, an Einstein glutamate pharmacologist /slash/ MILF lived there too and used to jog along its roads. Before she came to Einstein and began a long association with Mike Bennett, one of the most eminent neurobiologists at Einstein, Mike and I both ran a 5 k race in Central Park, sponsored by Pernod; my first 5k and my first taste of Pernod too. We did not vie for who would win the race, since I was passed by grandmothers and by ladies pushing strollers, and even Mike's Golden Retriever kept pace with him far, far ahead of me. No, the competition occurred later that day when we were at a bar and we both saw a young gal. I won that round. I suspect, but cannot prove, that he later got his revenge on me: A sultry, large-breasted female student and I both applied for the Woods Hole Neurobiology course one summer. I thought I was a shoo-in since I was going into neuroscience, whereas she was going into general surgery. Yet she was chosen and he was on the admission committee.

8th year: Lab studies with Lola Reid and external rotations at MGH and NIH

My MD-PhD program was supposed to be a six year accelerated program but I took an extra year to finish my retino-tectal studies, and yet another year to work with a new faculty member, Lola Reid, in what was essentially a postdoctoral fellowship while still a graduate student. Lola was from North Carolina, very ambitious and a bit unconventional (if she had been English you would have said that she was delightfully eccentric) but she was sweet and fiercely honest. She had been studying the differentiation of liver and other tissues in vitro on reconstituted basement membrane, prepared from the Engelbreth-Holm-Swarm (EHS) sarcoma which secreted massive amounts of basement membrane proteins. This tumor had to be grown in nude mice, which serendipitously Lola was maintaining in a separate line of studies. So, we decided to see what would happen if a retina was placed near a piece of EHS sarcoma in culture. (This experiment was modeled after the classic experiment of Rita Levi-Montalcini, in which she found that pieces of tissues secreting Nerve Growth Factor stimulated nerve growth.)

In fact, the EHS sarcoma, and purified laminin derived from this tumor, acted as fantastic substrates for nerve growth. Seeing this for the first time through the microscope was the biggest "Aha!" moment of my career. Some months later, having submitted an abstract at the Society for Neuroscience and presented the work to a packed auditorium in 1981, I thought that I had secured scientific priority on this seminal finding. The study of laminin in the nervous system blossomed into an entire field in the following years. But in fact, the scientific community credited a paper that came out the following year instead: Baron-Van Evercooren A, Kleinman HK, Ohno S, Marangos P, Schwartz JP, Dubois-Dalcq ME. Nerve growth factor, laminin, and fibronectin promote neurite growth in human fetal sensory ganglia cultures. J Neurosci Res. 1982;8(2-

3):179-93. Meanwhile, the paper that I wrote on retinal outgrowth on EHS sarcoma and laminin substrates did not appear until 1984. There's a story behind this....

Lola had received the EHS sarcoma from George R. Martin at the National Institutes of Health (NIH), who was the grand old man of the extracellular matrix field (his European counterpart being Rupert Timpl) and leader of a large laboratory. Lola offered George co-authorship on the paper we were writing and sent him a draft to comment upon. We waited for a reply – more than 6 months, perhaps more than 8 months. As I will tell in the following section, I did a rotation for two months in clinical genetics at the NIH campus in Bethesda during this time too, visiting Hynda Kleinman (George's right-hand), and George Martin too, both of whom were friendly, giving and helpful. Eventually, I believe Lola got nothing back from George other than a statement that he had no comments and did not need to be a co-author; my recollection is that this occurred right about the time that the Baron-Van Evercooren paper came out. Although nothing in this behavior constituted scientific misconduct, I learned the concept of "frenemy" for the first time, though not for the last.

My rotation in Boston, at Massachusetts General Hospital in child neurology, was a rude awakening since I was so far behind the other students in sucking-up skills, I mean, in presenting patients in a scholarly manner. The others followed the model of case presentations in the New England Journal of Medicine, giving long detailed discussions of differential diagnosis, citing the literature, and proposing a barrage of unnecessary tests to rule out all possible arcane causes. As the reader can attest, I love the arcane and scholarly as much as anyone, but when a simple definitive test is available, I would do that first before doing every other test in parallel. I should have realized that I was no academic child neurologist in the making! As it happens, my main memory of Boston was a night in the Combat Zone with Charlie Mick and Dave Rosenbaum; we got separated at one point, and in searching for one of them, I found that one of the strip club owners was also looking for him! Yikes.

The rotation at NIH was genteel but disorganized. A few studies of rare genetic diseases were underway at the Clinical Center, in which patients were brought in and studied in return for free medical care. Duties were pretty light (no all-nighters or emergency admissions) and I basically hung out. I wrote a case study which we never published (it described a patient who had two very rare conditions at once; but we could not rule out the possibility that they co-occurred by chance). As I mentioned, I also spent time with Hynda Kleinman in Martin's lab. The most important experience was buying an engagement ring and proposing to Sue on Valentine's Day, at Anna Maria's restaurant in Dupont Circle in DC. This turned out to be a mistake – not the wedding, har har, but buying the ring without her input and guidance. The setting stuck out too far and kept getting caught on things, and eventually Sue bought another ring (without my input and guidance) which suited her just fine.

Lesson learned – don't buy jewelry for someone unless they are within arm's reach of you.

Transitioning to postdoc and/or residency

As my time at Einstein began to draw to a close, I was torn between two possible paths: pursuing a postdoc in a laboratory or following a research-oriented residency first. I applied to a few outstanding laboratories and a few stellar residencies. Spoiler alert: I did not go to any of them.

My first inclination was to join the laboratory of Gerald Edelman at Rockefeller University. He had won the Nobel Prize in Immunology but had switched to Neuroscience and was doing cutting-edge, visionary research that I admired. He was having an affair with Liv Ullmann too, which impressed me as much as the Nobel Prize. My interview with him took place in his well-appointed office and went very well, although his last question to me was the most crucial: He wondered whether I would insist on studying my own topics, the correct answer being that I would work on whatever he wanted me to. I also interviewed several of his students, including Mike Greenberg and Urs Rutishauser, and got frank answers about the environment in the lab. I finally decided not to go, since I valued my independence more than the chance to learn from a master at first hand.

I also went to Vanderbilt University to interview with Stanley Cohen, another brilliant and inventive biochemist who had won the Nobel Prize for discovery of Epidermal Growth Factor and probably had deserved to share another one for Nerve Growth Factor. He was as down to earth as Edelman had been suave. To my surprise, he regarded me as a "mere" pediatrician (true, I had no prior experience in biochemistry) and his advice to me was to start by purifying EGF from liver tissue. Up til now, he had purified EGF from tumors or snake venom, and wanted to compare it to EGF from normal mammalian tissues. Again, as much as I liked him, I did not want to do someone else's study, even if it meant the chance to apprentice with one of my idols. His thick Brooklyn accent is still in my ears.

Meanwhile, I was also interviewing at a handful of research-oriented residencies. I should have known that I would not be a competitive candidate, since I did not get elected to the Honor Society and had not distinguished myself in clinical rotations. Yet I was chosen for interviews, presumably in view of my PhD, and I was optimistic. The most memorable interview was at UCSF. I had flown in from New York and rented a car, which I then took to Golden Gate Park to see the Exploratorium. When I returned to the car, I found that my luggage had been stolen from the trunk, leaving me with only jeans and t-shirt to wear to the interview. When I showed up and tried to explain that my clothes had just been stolen, I got blank stares, as if the interviewer were deaf. Lesson learned: Travel in your interview suit, just in case. There may be additional lessons to learn from this too.

How I wound up at the University of Chicago pediatrics residency: It was Match Day, the day when all the students across the nation, and all of the residency programs across the nation, compare the lists of student preferences and program preferences and try to make an optimal solution. I had only applied to two or three programs, and was not accepted to any. Coincidentally, the Chairman of the University of Chicago pediatrics department, Lawrence Gartner, was visiting Einstein (giving a talk on breast-feeding) and was shocked to learn that his department did not fill their quota either! Evidently their program had made some changes that made the current residents unhappy and they had bad-mouthed the program to candidates. Gartner's faculty host at Einstein was one of my mentors, and called me into his room to meet Larry. We were introduced and shook hands. He asked if I wanted to come to Chicago, and I said Sure.

Years later, as a tenure-track faculty member in his department, Gartner wrote me a letter of recommendation that said: "I personally recruited Neil to my department."

Chapter Five. Days in Chicago 1982-1996

Sue and I got married at a golf course in Connecticut, in pouring, drenching rain that lasted for days; honeymooned in Block Island; and then drove out to Chicago in her gold VW Beetle with sun-roof and her topaz-colored Cocker Spaniel. During the years 1982-1996, we bought an old fixer-upper house in Oak Park (1983) and filled it with three children, Daniel (1986), Adam (1988), and Emily (1991). Sue worked as Registered Nurse at Michael Reese Hospital and later as Nurse Educator at Hines VA Hospital. She does not know any of the music of the era because she was busy taking care of the three little ones!

Pediatrics at University of Chicago

My plan was to do one year of pediatrics as a prerequisite for doing a Neurology residency, ultimately to be a pediatric neurologist. Silly me. Pediatrics turned out to be asthma and sickle cell anemia, and pediatric neurology turned out to be seizures and developmental delay. I slowly realized that these experiences would have little synergy with, or give little insight into, laboratory studies of brain development. Perhaps the lowest point was rotating in the neonatal ICU and putting in an IV at 4 am on a tiny tot who was attempting to scream but only able to make feeble noises.

I was lucky enough to work alongside Diana Woo, a wise clinician who once cautioned me against ordering blood transfusions too liberally. Although AIDS had recently been described in case reports, its relation to blood transfusions had not become general knowledge yet in medical circles. I am still not sure whether she knew something or had a premonition. Diana died of cancer at an early age, but was so beloved that the department established a memorial lecture in neonatology in her name.

I also happened to observe two instances of medical mistakes, one by a nephrologist who mis-handled a patient with neurogenic hypertension, and one much more sinister because it was a systematic byproduct of the medical system. A child with developmental delay was referred to a clinic, and they proceeded to carry out a very systematic, thorough, multi-disciplinary work up involving half a dozen specialists. After weeks of testing the group got together to make a diagnostic and treatment plan. The trouble was, it was apparent at the outset that the patient had an enlarged head circumference, and it was getting larger and larger by the day as he was being sent from one specialist to the other. I was not able to get anyone's attention that they needed to hit the Pause button and deal with his urgent problem immediately.

Biochemical and cell biological studies with Nancy Schwartz

The department of pediatrics had an affiliated research institute, which specialized in extracellular matrix proteins and their associated genetic disorders. Nancy Schwartz, PhD, was youngish (around 40) but already had tenure, as well as hair that had turned completely grey. Her research concerned the structure and function of proteoglycans, which are proteins that have long chains of certain sugar structures attached to them. They are important for the functioning of extracellular matrix and how cells respond to their environment. The U of Chicago group had made hay from a tumor called chondrosarcoma, which secreted massive amounts of proteoglycans and hyaluronic acid, a felicitous source comparable to the EHS sarcoma that had been so fruitful in studying extracellular matrix proteins. So I felt at home.

Having recently shown that neurites (among other cells and cell protrusions) respond to laminin, I thought the next logical step was to identify the receptors on the surface of these neurites that interacted directly with laminin. Laminin was known to bind heparan sulfate, one of the types of sugar chains found on proteoglycans, so it was plausible that the laminin receptor might be a proteoglycan. I asked Nancy if I could spend a year on leave from the residency in her lab, looking for the receptor. She said Yes, which put her far ahead of any Nobel prize winner in my book. I applied for, and received, a NIH predoctoral fellowship which supported my work for two years.

Soon after I began my hunt for a laminin receptor, others found a family of extracellular matrix (ECM) receptors called the integrins. These bound laminin with relatively low affinity, whereas I believed that I was looking for a high affinity receptor. My strategy was to make laminin radioactive, then lay it over a blot consisting of size-separated proteins under conditions that would minimize nonspecific binding and maximize specific binding. This was yet another Aha! moment when I developed the autoradiogram and saw a discrete radioactive band at ~120 kiloDaltons (a measure of protein size).

I set out to isolate and characterize this protein, which I had facetiously called cranin in honor of Stan Crain. During this period, one of Nancy's technicians would walk past me in the hallway and mutter to me, "You're dead!", referring to the fact that I was not publishing anything and should just accept defeat. Eventually, I completed a paper that was accepted to the *Proceedings of the National Academy of Sciences* (a high-impact journal) and published in 1987. I had been appointed as Instructor, which is the lowest faculty level that would allow me to write grants; I was granted a five year FIRST award from NIH and was then promoted to Assistant Professor on the tenure track, beginning in 1988.

I was a bad project manager for running a laboratory. My side project while isolating cranin was to conduct a "kinetic analysis" of neurite growth in culture, which did lead to a long series of papers, but had relatively little impact on the field (studies of neurites in terms of cellular and molecular mechanisms were favored instead). I was also bad at hiring and training assistants. One time I hired a young guy who suffered from dyslexia and could not add or multiply two numbers, nor could he recognize his deficit.

Turns out that cranin was identical to another laminin binding protein called dystroglycan – but whereas dystroglycan had been thought to be a proteoglycan, I showed that it is, quite surprisingly, actually a mucin-like protein, with a different and unique type of sugar structures that are critical for its binding to laminin. There are even diseases where the defect is in the sugar structures, so they are important both biochemically and clinically. This work was published in two papers in *Journal of Biological Chemistry*, the top journal of the field. Yet it was too little too late for my promotion. I did not have a teaching portfolio to speak of, I was not contributing to service within the department (or outside either), and my FIRST award had expired and I had not won any new grants. I had gambled that a single-minded focus on my own research would prevail, and it didn't. So Nancy's technician had been right after all – I was dead.

It is not quite true that I did not obtain any new grants after my FIRST award ended. Partly in desperation, and partly to prove that I knew how to write grants, I wrote a grant entirely for cynical motives, that is, because I thought it followed a fundable formula. I found a recently published report in a high-impact journal that appeared to be "too good to be true", and proposed to replicate the work using better and more precise methods. I did get a two-year grant from a private foundation to see if Heat Shock Protein 60 is altered in the blood of subjects with schizophrenia. In retrospect this project was more of an unfortunate diversion rather than a lifesaver. We could not replicate the original finding, and I realized that publishing the negative result would be a waste of time and effort better spent on writing new grants on cranin. I had hoped that this grant would allow me to conduct pilot studies to find new fundable findings to follow up on, but my collaborator, a clinical psychiatrist, had a very narrow view of what a grant should be. Getting a new grant requires conducting preliminary studies which can only be supported by being piggybacked on other projects. As long as the pilot studies are related in some coherent fashion, this is expected and even encouraged by funders. However, in his view, spending grant funds on pilot studies was fiscal misconduct tantamount to spending the money on hookers and blow. This was a guy who was on the board of the local synagogue yet loved to eat shellfish – so who was he to talk?

In between U of C and UIC

I received a one-year terminal employment contract in 1995, which stimulated me to carry out a flurry of activities, trying to keep busy and trying to find new lines of research and employment. For example, I wrote a massive review called "Proteins in Unusual Locations" which synthesized disparate studies showing that, for example, proteins thought to function within the nucleus also could be expressed on the cell surface, and vice versa. Using a series of antibodies that I had raised against cranin/dystroglycan (and commercialized by the way; the U of C still sends me royalties), I proceeded to do collaborations with a variety of colleagues from around the country, such as Ben Peng and Mike Gershon. I visited Linda Van Eldik's laboratory and did pilot studies to see if the response of cultured astrocytes to amyloid beta-peptide was modified by laminin. I wrote a variety of colleagues from my past and present asking for advice or leads on employment, but those who bothered to reply were noncommittal or were frankly not encouraging.

Walter Pitts

Perhaps the most cathartic activity that I undertook at this time was a project to find biographical information on Walter Pitts. As an undergraduate, the paper "What the Frog's Eye tells the Frog's Brain" by Jerome Lettvin and his team (especially Walter Pitts and Warren McCulloch) seemed to me the pinnacle both of brain research and of scientific writing. In my mind, Lettvin was a Nobel contender of the stature of David Hubel and Torsten Wiesel, who actually did win the Nobel prize. Lettvin had a long iconoclastic career at MIT, and his wife Maggie was a minor celebrity because she had an exercise show on public television (ironic that she was so fit when Lettvin was the epitome of a couch potato). I went to New Jersey and interviewed Jerry Lettvin and a few of his colleagues including Jerome Wiesner, the former dean of MIT who had recruited McCulloch, Lettvin and Pitts to MIT in the 1950s.

Walter Pitts was a mysterious, legendary prodigy who had run away from home at age 15 and started hanging around at U of Chicago, first studying under the logician

Carnap and later collaborating with Warren McCulloch, whose laboratory at UIC was in the basement of the Neuropsychiatric Institute. (Factoid: the building is situated where left field was in the original Cubs stadium.) McCulloch was a hard-drinking bohemian -- one of his lovers was Margaret Mead -- who attracted, even collected, an eclectic assortment of eccentric and troubled individuals, who often stayed with him and his wife on their farm in New England. Scientifically, he combined a systematic mainstream experimental program with more speculative theoretical studies. The paper that Pitts wrote with Warren McCulloch created the entire idea of the brain as a digital network of all-or-none firing neurons, i.e., the brain as a digital computer. This paper was published in a local, obscure U of Chicago-based journal called *Bulletin of Mathematical Biophysics*, but was hailed as a true breakthrough both for brain science as well as computer science. John von Neumann cited this paper as the basis for his design for the digital computer.

Jerry Lettvin was a medical student working with McCulloch, and he and Walter spent so many hours talking and brainstorming in Jerry's dorm room that they were suspected of being gay lovers. Their response, or "revenge", was to explain that they were working on a scientific paper. Pitts wrote, apparently tongue-in-cheek, a mathematical model of mood disorders, which not only was published and taken seriously but which presaged the entire field of computational psychiatry.

Lettvin's career arc took him from a neurology residency at Boston City Hospital, to an appointment at Manteno State Hospital in rural Illinois, where he established a research lab that attracted collaborators from around the world, and finally to MIT, when the entire McCulloch/Lettvin/Pitts group was reunited with high hopes. No one got very close to Walter, even his few friends, but there are tales of long road trips to and from Mexico, which have faint echoes of "On the Road". When hiking, Walter would take books along with him and throw away each page as he read it. At MIT, Walter became a protégé of Norbert Wiener, whose book "Cybernetics" launched the field of using feedback and feedforward control techniques, applied to diverse applications ranging from precision bomb targeting to robotics and brain modeling.

Throughout his life, Walter never earned any degrees (he was the kind of guy who would challenge the exam with questions of his own) and had no faculty appointments. He had stayed in the shadow of three famous scientists (McCulloch, Lettvin, and Wiener) all of whom, "coincidentally", did their best work during the time they collaborated with him. My kind of guy, clearly! Unfortunately, after a falling out with Wiener over a family dispute, Walter began a long, slow decline. Paychecks piled up, unopened and uncashed. Walter became a sad, lonely alcoholic sitting in bars nursing a beer and nursing a book, dying while still a young man.

Even though Walter had had an unhappy end, perhaps counter-intuitively this project helped me feel much better about myself and the scientific enterprise in general. I had since found a new faculty appointment at UIC and was busy with forward-looking projects, so the paper on Pitts was not submitted for publication for several more years.

Chapter Six. UIC part 1: 1996-2000

Joining the Costa group at UIC

Erminio Costa was frustrated because, unlike his buddies Paul Greengard and Gerry Edelman, he had not won the Nobel Prize. He had made several breakthroughs, including elucidating the mechanisms by which benzodiazepine drugs work to reduce anxiety and promote sleep. These include Xanax and Valium, for example, and they work by modulating the so-called GABA-A receptor. But whereas Greengard was at Yale and Edelman at Rockefeller University, Costa's appointments had been less prestigious and he had raised himself by his bootstraps. (He started at U of Caligari, and worked in the IL State Psychiatric Hospital in Galesburg, IL, but became famous during his time running a large laboratory first at St. Elizabeth's Hospital in Washington, DC as part of the National Institute for Mental Health, then across town at Georgetown University.) And whereas Gerry had a well-publicized affair with a Swedish movie star, who even wrote about him in her memoir, Erminio was rumored to have a *sub rosa* longtime relationship with a quiet, studious neuroscientist.

Costa departed Georgetown when one of his funders, an Italian pharmaceutical company named Fidia, went bankrupt under shady circumstances, and he had recently landed at UIC in Chicago. There was some irony in this because the Head of Psychiatry who hired him, Boris Astrachan, shrewdly did so with the explicit understanding that he would work on schizophrenia, a devastating yet relatively common disease that had resisted much progress. Ironic because Costa had openly mocked schizophrenia researchers as wasting their time on a disease that was not ripe for study, while he, Costa was smart enough to reap the benefits of the much more fertile field of molecular pharmacology.

I did not know much personally about Costa at the time, but when I heard that he had moved to Chicago, I wrote him a letter asking if we could meet and explore mutual interests. We met and he led me through a free-wheeling, far-reaching interview about diverse scientific and non-scientific topics, which was strikingly similar to the interview that Edelman had led me through. He agreed to find a position for me and would propose me for a tenure-track assistant professorship in his group.

His friends called him Mimo. I called him Doctor Costa.

I arrived in the laboratory three months early, as an unpaid visitor, and spent the time brainstorming possible projects. This rubbed across the grain of Costa's philosophy, which was to get started doing experiments first and see where they evolved. Although I had been hired with the understanding that I would join the tenure track, Costa said that UIC would not approve this; he did have open tenure-track positions though and hired two others soon after I arrived. A charitable explanation is that he thought I seemed too lost and rootless to make it. An alternative hypothesis is that he had me trapped and could conserve his resources. Regardless, having no options and being an incurable optimist, I stayed.

The reelin story

Almost when I arrived at UIC, Costa did two things that I thought were brilliant:

The first was to jump on a possible animal model of schizophrenia: The *reeler* mutation altered development in the forebrain (and other regions) and made a mouse that was "weird". Certainly the forebrain controls higher brain functions which are disturbed in schizophrenia, but Costa immediately made the hypothesis that a deficiency of reelin (the protein lost in the reeler mutation) is the cause of schizophrenia. From one point of view, this was a Hail-Mary pass, a leap in the dark, but actually, it made perfect sense from another perspective: Reelin was the first gene identified at the molecular and gene-sequence level that controlled forebrain development. Thus, one could test conclusively whether the hypothesis was true or not! And if in fact the hypothesis was true, they would have a huge breakthrough in understanding the disease. And if not, as I mentioned, Costa believed in getting started and seeing where the results lead.

The second brilliant decision was to devise a better, more quantitative method for measuring levels of the reelin gene products, coupling hypothesis testing with new methods development. Over the history of neuroscience, new tools have been arguably more effective than new ideas in enabling leaps of progress.

The microelectrode, the fMRI machine, and the electron microscope are but three examples of this. True, my own forte is in the realm of ideas, but developing new methods are a better bet nonetheless.

Over the next five years, Costa and his dozen-odd students and collaborators developed the reelin hypothesis of schizophrenia, carried out lots of experimental studies, and tried unsuccessfully to get a big Center grant funded by NIH. This research project has been told elsewhere (Guidotti A, Auta J, Chen Y, Davis JM, Dong E, Gavin DP, Grayson DR, Matrisciano F, Pinna G, Satta R, Sharma RP, Tremolizzo L, Tueting P. Epigenetic GABAergic targets in schizophrenia and bipolar disorder. Neuropharmacology. 2011 Jun;60(7-8):1007-16. doi: 10.1016/j.neuropharm.2010.10.021) but since this book is about m-o-i, I will just mention the activities that involved yours truly.

At the time, it was thought that reelin was only expressed in a few specialized cells in the developing brain. However, I realized that reelin is an extracellular matrix protein and almost all such proteins are expressed widely in multiple tissues. In particular, if reelin is found in the blood of adult humans, one could measure it in subjects with schizophrenia. I developed an assay to measure reelin protein and showed that it was not only found in blood, but in a variety of places in the body (e.g., the liver, chromaffin cells of the adrenal gland, etc.) which potentially might secrete reelin. I did get two small grants related to this effort, one to develop and validate the assay, and one to examine expression of reelin in the blood of autistic individuals. We found that the expression of reelin did vary according to the gene structure of the individual, which was interesting because others had shown that a variant gene structure tended to occur in autistics. This was probably my major contribution to Costa's group. Investigators are still studying and publishing papers on reelin protein in human diseases to this day.

I was encouraged to write a grant that would test whether reelin protein in the blood was affected in schizophrenia, and Costa told me to write it, then left for six months on sabbatical. When he returned, he claimed that he had never told me to write it. I suspect that he did not want to do any experiment that might give a negative result, which would put a monkey-wrench into his attempt to get the Center funded, even if the negative result could be explained away later. Maybe he had figured that I would never get it together enough to actually write and submit it without him. In any case, he forced me to withdraw the already-submitted proposal from consideration at NIH, and lodged a formal complaint against me that said I had received unpublished data under false pretenses from his right-hand man, Alessandro Guidotti, to include in the proposal. Fortunately, John Davis, the most eminent professor in the department and a former director of the Institute, backed me up and verified that Costa had directly told me to write the grant in front of the entire group in a lab meeting.

Another potential tissue source of reelin, that can be sampled from adult humans, is to biopsy the nasal epithelium. I submitted and got Institutional Review Board approval to obtain nasal epithelium from healthy individuals – people undergoing nose jobs had some of this tissue removed and discarded anyway. However, Dr. Costa proceeded to tell me that I was to give the tissue to George Pappas to process and analyze. Remember George Pappas? My old professor from Einstein had become chairman of Anatomy and Cell Biology at UIC and was collaborating with Costa. Speaking of noses, the idea that I would willingly give away my hard-earned nasal epithelium made me snort out of my own nose. This appeared to be punishment for being too independent (even though, remember, I was also supposed to achieve independence). Or perhaps this simply meant that Costa did not believe I was competent to carry out my own experiments.

The Costa lab did show that the expression of reelin mRNA was decreased by about half in the brains of individuals dying from schizophrenia. In fact, this finding has been replicated quite well by many laboratories. At one of the group lab meetings, I mentioned that the *reeler* heterozygote mouse also has half the normal amount of reelin, so maybe it could serve as an animal model of schizophrenia. Costa was vociferous in denouncing me for raising this stupid idea. This is why he was the big cheese and I was a little nothing – he would never follow such a line of investigation as that.

After the Center proposal had been reviewed by NIH for the first time, the "pink sheets" were released which contained the critiques of the reviewers. One of the reviewers made a snarky comment: "If the reelin hypothesis is correct, then heterozygote mice which have one copy of the reelin gene should show some of the features of schizophrenia." The reviewer meant this sarcastically, since previous anatomical studies had suggested that heterozygote animals were completely normal. However, Costa saw this as a critical test of the hypothesis and proceeded to characterize very carefully the behavior and biochemistry of the heterozygote mouse. In fact, these studies eventually became the centerpoint of his research. I was certainly not part of this project, nor was my original suggestion acknowledged; nor did he ever apologize or admit he was wrong in his original assessment. After all, he had been right all along: He was still the big cheese and I was a little nothing.

As I alluded, Costa never did get his NIH Center grant funded. He gave a talk to the Institute in which he basically said, "this was all your fault and fuck you all". Then he retreated to his own lab and his own personal grants, and was Institute director only in name.

I will leave you with just one more bit of drama. In one meeting, I saw Costa angrily grab Hari Manev (see below) by his shirt in a threatening manner. This was actually mild behavior since he had been known in past years for throwing chairs. Regardless, I wrote a letter to the department Head, Joe Flaherty, reporting this and saying I felt that I was in an unsafe workplace. I am particularly proud of one line in this letter: "I would take a bullet <u>for</u> him, but I won't take a bullet <u>from</u> him." I never heard any follow-up regarding that letter, which I am sure was placed quietly in a personnel file, yet I am also sure that Flaherty did not forget it. He was the kind of person who kept his powder dry.

<u>Finding my own projects</u>

During the period when the group as a whole, and me in particular, were working on reelin, I was also exploring various possible research directions which might support me to become an independently funded investigator and get back on the tenure-track.

One line of work seemed promising. I had noticed that the antidepressant fluoxetine (a.k.a. Prozac) was reported to stimulate production of a protein called BDNF in the brain. At the same time, others had reported that BDNF stimulates production of new neurons (neurogenesis) in the dentate gyrus of adult rats and mice. Putting these two ideas together, I hypothesized that fluoxetine might stimulate neurogenesis. I went to my colleague Hari Manev to see if we could test this.

Hari had been a student of Costa's some years back, then had moved to Medical College of Pennsylvania. He had tenure, but the entire medical school declared bankruptcy and merged with Hahnemann Medical College. Somewhere along the line, he lost his appointment – the take home lesson being that there is no end of ways to be terminated even when you have tenure! (This might be a good time to mention that the gadfly philosopher Charles Peirce was removed from Harvard by dissolving the entire department that he was in, and forming a new department that rehired everyone but him.) When Costa came to UIC, he was one of the people that Costa recruited to join him. Like me, his options were limited; unlike me, I believe he was hired as a full professor.

Hari agreed to treat rats with fluoxetine. We injected them with a drug, BrdU, which gets incorporated into dividing cells, and served as a marker of neurogenesis. I counted BrdU-containing neurons in the dentate gyrus, while Hari's wife, Rada, and his postdoc, Tolga Uz, did other aspects of the project. We found that chronic, but not acute, treatment with fluoxetine caused a huge increase in neurogenesis in the dorsal dentate (note that depressive symptoms respond to chronic, but not acute antidepressant treatment). Seeing the labeled neurons in the dentate in the microscope was another Aha! moment.

When we presented the results to Costa, he was indifferent and uninterested in this as a potential line of work. I suspect that he mainly did not want to dilute our efforts, which he felt should be entirely focused on getting his Center funded. In any case, we put the data in a drawer for several years, until Hari in disgust decided to write it up and submit a short paper regardless of Costa's approval. This paper became highly cited even though two or three other groups published the same finding at about the same time. Hari, being more independent of Costa than I was, wrote and got a grant to study fluoxetine and neurogenesis. This research area has subsequently blossomed into an entire field, as researchers have asked: Is stimulated neurogenesis critical for antidepressant drugs to be clinically effective? Is depressed neurogenesis a cause or risk factor for clinical depression? Will fluoxetine stimulate learning and memory, or other aspects of brain function that involve neurogenesis?

Perhaps the lowest point in my efforts to find a suitable line of independent research was when I decided to see whether cocaine would disrupt forebrain development in fetal rats. Specifically, I treated pregnant rats with cocaine at a specific time window in pregnancy, expecting to selectively disrupt migration of neurons to the most advanced part of the forebrain. To do this pilot study, one of Costa's postdocs had placed chronic, indwelling catheters in the subclavian vein of a half-dozen pregnant rats, who were housed in the VA Hospital about half a mile from my building. Pregnant rats are much like ferrets in size and like dogs in personality; they have definite personalities, look directly at you, and hug you as you hold them. I obtained cocaine from Sandro Guidotti (who kept it locked in a safe) and carried the cocaine, in syringes, together with a box of supplies, as I trudged miserably for the half mile through blowing snow. Did I mention this was in the middle of winter in Chicago? Then, one by one, I pushed the cocaine through the cannula of each rat. When the cocaine hits the brain, the rat acts crazy and runs around in a frenzy, so I had to hurry to return it to its cage. Each time the rat was injected, it became more and more sensitized to the effects of cocaine, so the frenzy would grow greater day by day. A few times, the pregnant rats would leap from my arms and I had to chase them around the room. After their babies were born, I sacrificed the offspring and cut sections through their forebrains, to count migrating neurons. This took another six months. After all that, I found nothing of interest!

Chapter Seven. Don Swanson and Arrowsmith

When I was at U of C, I was a regular reader of the essays that were published in the in-house U of C journal called *Perspectives in Biology and Medicine*. Mostly these essays were on medical, medical-philosophical or medical-ethical topics, but a series of three papers that appeared in 1986, 1988 and 1990, from Don Swanson, who was Dean of the Graduate Library School, impressed me at the time. The first paper argued that fish oil may be regarded as a potential treatment for Raynaud's disease (a disorder in which small arteries undergo spasm, leading for example to cold fingers that can even exhibit frostbite), even though no single study had ever examined this question explicitly, because fish oil was reported to exert multiple physiological effects in the opposite direction from the pathophysiological alterations seen in Raynaud's disease. The second paper did a similar analysis for magnesium as a putative treatment for migraine headaches. Although no one had ever examined this question experimentally or clinically, and only one person had raised the possibility in print, Don pointed out that there were multiple physiological processes affected by magnesium, which were in the opposite direction from pathophysiological changes seen in migraine headaches. These two articles are now regarded as classics of information science and launched the field of "literature based discovery". (The third paper, on somatomedin-C and arginine, has not held up as well over time.)

Just to clarify the term, as it is generally used, "undiscovered public knowledge" refers to the fact that information may be published and yet no one may be aware of it! There are various reasons why this may happen; the article may be published in an obscure journal or hard to find (e.g., not available except on the shelves of a special library), people may not have bothered to read it, or indeed those who have read it may not be alive anymore or may not remember it. I mentioned earlier an example where the answer to David Soll's final exam was sitting on library shelves but no one in the class knew how to find it (except by random luck). I will give another example of this in my own research later on as well.

"Literature based discovery" (LBD) is a particularly interesting type of "undiscovered public knowledge" which refers to the process of assembling separate assertions that are located in disparate documents. These may be found in different journals, different disciplines, and different times, and potential new knowledge is created by putting them together to form a new assertion that is novel and scientifically interesting, i.e., worth testing experimentally or clinically. For example, the assertion or finding "A affects B" may be found in one paper, and "B affects C" in another; the assertion "A affects C" is presented to the user who may (or may not) decide that it is scientifically meaningful, nontrivial, and worth studying. As one can imagine, the potential number of combinations of assertions in the scientific literature is astronomical, so the art/science of LBD is to identify and rank or filter the most promising "needles" out of a huge potential "haystack".

Don called me sometime in 1992 (or was it 1993?) to ask me about a possible artifact in his ongoing studies. In short, magnesium seemed to be linked to every disease in neurology! How could this be? I explained that magnesium was a regulator of the NMDA channel, and that excessive stimulation of this channel was a cause of excitotoxicity, which is a central mechanism of pathophysiology in stroke and many other diseases. As well, magnesium can antagonize the effects of calcium, and calcium influxes via various channels is again, a prevalent theme in neuronal functions. We started working together, in what became a garage-band type of informal collaboration, not too dissimilar from writing "Standard Deviations" with Ritchie.

Don was a big-nosed, thin, fit guy in his mid-70s who ran long distances passionately (though never entire marathons). He had a shelf of trophies in his office (I always went to his office, never he to mine) and explained that the older he got, the easier it was to win in his age bracket. He was regarded as one of the pioneers of information science, having been responsible for computerizing the Library of Congress, and mentored a generation of students who were to go on to be leaders in information science. Though Dean of the Graduate Library School, this entity was dissolved by U of C, which had decided that librarianship was not a sexy enough discipline and definitely not the wave of the future. Don had been married four times, twice to his current wife Patricia. Besides his regular articles, he also wrote a series of critiques on psychoanalysis, including a satirical piece on conducting psychoanalysis on dead persons. And last but not least, he suffered from both Raynaud's disease and migraine headaches, which had motivated him to carry out searches of the medical literature. (Years later, he would carry out searches on atrial fibrillation and long distance running, an important topic since his chronic atrial fibrillation eventually caused him to have multiple strokes which ended his career.)

We wrote a paper on magnesium and neurologic diseases in 1994, followed by three more LBD analyses which appeared as brief papers in leading neurology and psychiatry journals in 1996 and 1998. Perhaps more importantly, I had helped Don to systematize his manual literature searches into formalized procedures that could be carried out by a computer. We called this strategy "Arrowsmith", after the heroic medical researcher in the novel by Sinclair Lewis. The so-called One Node Search applied when the user has a known problem but is searching for a promising possible (unknown) solution. The Two Node Search applied when the user has a finding or hypothesis that links two items (e.g., concepts, entities, research areas) and seeks to analyze the various ways that they are linked, to see whether the existing literature supports studying that link further. Don was originally focused primarily on the One Node Search, but I felt that scientists would use the Two Node Search far more often. Our paper on Arrowsmith was published in a special issue of *Artificial Intelligence* and became our most cited work (more than 600 citations to date). By this time I had moved from U of C (which tolerated but did not appreciate my sidetrack into informatics) to UIC.

What do you think Costa thought of my garage band project? If you have been reading this book from the beginning, and not jumping around at random, you will infer that Costa did not find any promise or merit at all in this total waste of time. I told him that I was simply doing this in my spare time, like writing poetry, and I did not expect him to approve.

Just as Don had called me out of the blue, so did another call arrive one day from Ron Kostoff, a program officer at the Office of Naval Research, who wondered if we would carry out a one-year demonstration project to show that LBD could benefit the intelligence community. He invited us to write a grant on some topic -- we chose bioterrorism and viruses. What he did not tell us was that he had already gotten an internal grant and was subcontracting the actual work to us. So we were in the nice position of writing a grant that we had already gotten. We ranked viruses in terms of their "actionability" for repurposing as airborne agents, that is, whether their genomes had been sequenced and whether they could be aerosolized. The list we generated agreed well with an intelligence-based list generated by an expert in the field.

The collateral byproduct of having an active ONR grant was that I was legit – that is, I could work on LBD not as a poet in my spare time, but as a faculty member on the clock. That meant that I could also prepare and write my own NIH grant to develop and evaluate Arrowsmith. As it happened, program officers at NIH had also wanted to support Don, but he was so unfamiliar with writing NIH proposals that his one attempt had not followed the basic format at all; for example, he wrote a Statement of Work (which is appropriate for contracts) rather than a Specific Aims section appropriate for grants. Long story short, I wrote and obtained a standard R01 grant (on the first attempt) to develop Arrowsmith and evaluate it using a group of neuroscience field testers. Actually, not a standard grant; whereas a standard grant is capped at $500,000 direct costs per year, my grant was in the Human Brain Project portfolio (co-funded by National Library of Medicine and National Institute for Mental Health) and I was given $600,000 per year for five years!

Getting a R01 grant from NIH is the standard bellwether for saying that an academic has "arrived" in the field. So finally, almost twenty years after graduating, and four years after being declared dead at U of C, I had my foot in the door again. I was smart enough to hire a right-hand man with a strong background in math, statistics, operations research and programming, namely, Vetle Torvik, who had just graduated from Louisiana State with a PhD, after having gotten a master's in Oregon and a bachelor's degree from St. Olaf College in Minnesota. Did I mention that he was 101% Norwegian? Although he was hired to be a project manager, he was inept at that and so I took on that role, allowing him to do what he did best – optimize things. Later he has established his own group at U of Illinois at Champaign-Urbana, at the best information science school in the country, where he has recently received tenure. I was also lucky enough to sign up Maryann Martone as one of the neuroscience field testers; at the time, she was assistant director of a Microscopy technology center at University of California-San Diego, and her sub-contract with me was the first NIH grant that she obtained in her own name. Later she became one of the grand-dames of the field of neuroinformatics, for example, principal investigator of the Neuroscience Information Framework (NIF), Chairman of the Board of the International Neuroscience Coordinating Facility, and so on. As for Don, he agreed to participate in the project but only as a sub-contractor. He always saw me as a neuroscience domain expert, and not as a colleague in information science. This was fair since I had taken no courses and read no articles on the subject! He did not want to be responsible for anything other than his own research work, which again, was fair.

What do you think Costa thought of my garage band project *now*? Actually, he said nothing at all to me. My grant funds were considered part of the Psychiatric Institute and he got credit and bonuses based on the aggregate grants that went to the Institute. Factoid: Steve Koslow, the program officer in charge of the Human Brain Project and my mentor before and after applying for the Arrowsmith grant, was an ex-student of Costa. Is it possible that Costa had informally put in a good word for me? Did Koslow want to stick it to Costa by helping me? I have no idea.

Chapter Eight. UIC part 2: Neuroscience studies

Once I received a R01 grant, two things happened. I was given an appointment on the tenure-track (still as an assistant professor), and my department Head, Joe Flaherty, gave me a suite of rooms on the fifth floor of the Psychiatric Institute building, outside the space allocated to the Costa group. I still maintained a wet-lab on the second floor as part of Costa's Institute. Now began a period lasting more than a decade in which I juggled two active laboratories, one in molecular neuroscience and one in informatics.

Joe Flaherty was an unlikely mentor for me. Tall, assertive, and handsome despite some pock-marks on his face, he had more than a little bit of shark in him, and was a consummate Machiavellian political manipulator. I think if I had been a career-ist I would have been lost in his department. However, he appreciated the fact that I did not have a political bone in my body and was totally focused on scholarship and science. Once, he walked past my lab and overhead a staff meeting in which I was explaining to my team what hermeneutics is all about. Also, it was his job to clean up after Costa's messes. So I have Joe to thank that I got my tenure-track position, and that I got my informatics lab. A few years later, when he himself had been promoted to Dean of the Medical School, he continued to support my tenure package and promotion. Joe had been angling to become Vice President for Health Affairs; but turns out the University president unexpectedly resigned due to a minor scandal, and the new president, Michael Hogan, brought in another guy instead. Joe responded by retiring from UIC and becoming Dean of the Medical School in Dominica, in the Caribbean! Sue and I unexpectedly ran into him in Miami Beach, where he lived and commuted to Dominica, tan, fit and smiling.

RNA interference

After having discussed all the flailing around that I did trying to find a promising line of research in neuroscience, it was only *after* getting the Arrowsmith grant that I stumbled onto one!

It all happened during an Institute seminar in which Hari Manev presented his new line of work, which he was hoping would blossom into a long-term project: Namely, he proposed to combine fruit fly (*Drosophila*) genetics, which was a powerful tool in molecular biology, with traditional pharmacology – he injected drugs into the abdomen of the fruit fly, much like you would inject drugs into the peritoneum of the rat or mouse! This was a neat, mind-blowing concept, one that you might expect to hear while passing around a doobie in a dorm room, not at a seminar! And not only would he inject drugs, but he would inject double-stranded RNA molecules that encoded specific genes. These were taken up and caused down-regulation of the fly's own gene, not only in the abdomen, but spread throughout the entire body, including the brain and even into the germline, so that the suppression would affect the offspring as well. This doubly mind-blowing phenomenon, called RNA interference, involved cutting up of the long RNA into small double-stranded pieces about 22 nucleotides long (called siRNAs), by an enzyme called Dicer. A few years later, the discovery of RNA interference would be awarded the Nobel prize, for work done in C. elegans, a type of worm. In fact, one could simply feed the worms bacteria that had been engineered to express double-stranded RNA, and this would be sufficient to suppress the worm's own gene throughout its body, including into the germline.

As Hari was presenting this background information, Costa piped up and said that this reminded him of the earlier work of James McConnell, who had trained flatworms to react to light and then ground-up the trained worms and fed them to naïve worms, who learned this task more quickly. And I remembered that McConnell's studies suggested that the active factor transferred to the naïve worms was a type of RNA. This triggered yet another Aha! moment.

I proceeded to write a paper, which proposed that the almost-forgotten studies of McConnell in the 1950s to 1970s might actually have been studying RNA interference after all. Furthermore, I proposed that double-stranded RNAs might be formed in the mammalian brain at the onset of learning, and that siRNAs might be involved in regulating normal learning and memory. This was published in a leading journal, *Trends in Neuroscience*, in 2001 with Hari and Costa as co-authors.

About a year later, I was contacted by Jonathan Pollock, a program officer at the National Institute on Drug Abuse, encouraging me to submit a grant to a special NIH CEBRA program intended for high-risk ideas. This was the second time that a program officer had reached out to me proactively. I strongly encourage scientists to at least discuss their ideas with program officers before writing or submitting their proposals, both to gauge their interest and to get invaluable advice along the way. The CEBRA grant started a laboratory project which was supplemented by several other small grants and lasted roughly fifteen years (2002-2015).

Hari did find NIH funding for his inject-the-fruit-fly-belly project, but only for two years. Although he had several further grants on other topics, he became discouraged and retired (too early, in my opinion). He moved back to his homeland of Croatia, and has undertaken a second career writing a series of science fiction novellas that combine scientific premises with allegorical / philosophical / satirical themes.

miRNAs and siRNAs

The molecular biologists were not amused by my proposal that RNA interference might be occurring in the normal mammalian brain. Experimentally, people had failed to find siRNAs in mammalian tissues, and theoretically, there were all sorts of reasons that this phenomenon should not occur. (A decade later, I wrote a review article, listing the objections and showing how each of them had failed to hold up over time.) Instead, hundreds of different types of small *single*-stranded RNAs had been discovered in normal tissues, of the same size as siRNAs (~22 nucleotides), formed by a different kind of precursor RNA structure (a hairpin instead of a linear double-strand), yet still formed by the cleavage activity of dicer. These so-called microRNAs (or miRNAs) regulated other RNAs by binding them (usually only a partial match) and having more limited, graded effects compared to siRNAs. My pragmatic response to this explosion of research progress in the field was to focus my lab's experiments initially not on siRNAs, but rather on the enzyme dicer, which is common to both siRNA and miRNA pathways.

I have promised that I will not provide a detailed retrospective of my scientific career, but we learned a lot from studying miRNAs and siRNAs over fifteen years! These fall into six different lines of investigation:

1. Bioinformatics studies of miRNA sequences.

Vetle knew nothing about biology, much less microRNAs. I knew less than nothing, which is to say, I was suspicious that much of the accepted information about microRNAs was wrong. For example, in the case of miRNAs, the first examples that were discovered had sequences that were highly conserved across species, so biologists were already expecting that all miRNAs should be highly conserved. The first examples of miRNA targeting other RNAs involved imperfect binding of the miRNA to the target RNA, which was a messenger RNA (mRNA) encoding a protein, and the effect was to reduce production of the protein rather than to decrease the abundance of the mRNA. So, biologists were already expecting that miRNAs would always target this type of RNA in this way.

This pitfall occurs often in science – one might say, it occurs routinely! -- when a phenomenon is originally discovered in a particular context, and scientists extrapolate from the original finding more quickly and widely than they should. Even more than routinely: After a significant new discovery is made, you can anticipate the march of follow-up high-impact papers that not only flesh it out in new domains, but that correct the mis-apprehensions and extrapolations that were initially made. So really, you can divide attention-getting papers into those that present something new (previously unexplored), and those that are surprising because they show that some previously accepted finding had been mis- or over-interpreted.

Vetle and I dealt with the uncertainty about microRNAs by taking an unbiased large scale statistical approach that made minimal assumptions about the rules governing them. We made a list of known microRNAs and scanned the entire database of (potential target) RNA sequences to tabulate the length of perfect binding that each miRNA sequence could exhibit across all targets. We then did this for randomly shuffled miRNA sequences, to serve as a baseline. The difference in binding interactions between real and shuffled miRNAs grew larger as the length of the binding region grew larger. That is, real miRNAs tended to bind large regions of potential target RNAs much more than could be accounted for by chance. In fact, we found some miRNAs that showed perfect binding to mRNAs, which led us to the discovery that a whole set of microRNAs in humans and other mammals were generated from a particular type of so-called junk DNA repeats. This took the field by surprise and the genomic repeat paper is our second highest cited (over 300 citations). In retrospect, the finding can be considered an example of "undiscovered public knowledge" since the public Genome Web Browser already overlaid these microRNA loci with annotated genomic repeats, and anyone who bothered to look could have discerned the pattern for themselves. A further analysis strongly predicted that another set of microRNAs are targeting another type of junk DNA repeat called Alu, which is very abundant in the human genome, and which inserts itself into many mRNAs that encode protein, where it can take on normal regulatory functions.

2. Dicer in the nervous system.

Dicer was already reasonably well characterized as a protein (it was available as a purified recombinant protein), and enzyme activity assays (known as RNAse III assays) had been well studied. We made an antibody against dicer, which we used to examine whether dicer is expressed in the adult mouse brain. We used four techniques to show that dicer is present: Western blots, which show the size of protein bands that bind dicer antibodies; immunocytochemistry, which shows the distribution of dicer protein spatially within slices of brain; immunoprecipitation, which brings down selectively proteins that bind dicer antibody (this can also bring down proteins that bind dicer, depending on the conditions used); and finally, electron microscopic immunocytochemistry, which shows where dicer protein is located at the subcellular level.

All of the lab studies of dicer and microRNAs were performed with Giovanni Lugli. Giovanni had arrived from Modena, Italy, having been under the impression that he had completed a doctorate. I enjoyed working with Giovanni since he was scrupulously honest, loyal, and scientifically fearless. He did not mind working on hypotheses that went against the grain of the mainstream. I proposed him for promotion from Research Associate to Research Assistant Professor, but this was blocked because it turned out that he had not actually earned a doctorate; rather, his university had attested that his graduate work "was the equivalent of" a doctorate. So, Giovanni enrolled at UIC and became my PhD student at the same time as we were working together on the dicer/microRNA/siRNA projects.

It was easy to demonstrate that dicer protein is expressed in the brain, particularly in large neurons, and particularly in parts of the brain that are involved in learning, memory, and so-called neural plasticity. However, when we tested immuno-purified dicer from mouse brain for enzymatic activity, we could not detect any activity at all! This quandary clarified itself when I brought together two separate lines of investigation: On the one hand, it was well known by molecular biologists that partially digesting dicer with proteases could greatly enhance its enzymatic activity, by generating active fragments. (There is a domain within the full-length dicer protein that masks or inhibits the activity of another domain, and the latter is unmasked when dicer is cleaved into pieces by proteases.) On the other hand, it was well known by neuroscientists that a protease called calpain is activated during synaptic stimulation that raises levels of calcium within neurons. I put these two together and hypothesized that synaptic stimulation might activate calpain and this calpain might cleave dicer, unmasking its RNAse III activity (which is required to generate miRNAs and siRNAs).

In short, we were able to confirm this hypothesis. Not only is dicer present in neurons and activated by synaptic stimulation, but dicer is highly enriched at the postsynaptic face of the excitatory synapse itself. Moreover, we found that microRNAs and especially their precursors are also highly enriched at the postsynaptic face, so that they would be in close proximity to dicer which would be in a great position to convert them to active miRNAs. These studies were nontrivial since, although the neuroscience community believed that microRNAs were expressed in neurons, the prevalent thinking was that they are generated in the cell body of the neuron. It was a big surprise to find the entire machinery is also localized at the synapse itself.

3. Exosomes, RNAs, and a new kind of cellular communication in the nervous system.

As you may be starting to discern, quite a few of my scientific insights arose from literature-based discovery-like reasoning, in which I juxtaposed threads from different fields and made new hypotheses out of them.

In 2007, a paper appeared in *Nature Cell Biology* which immediately drew my attention. Small vesicles called exosomes, secreted by cells into the blood or other extracellular fluids, were already known to contain a variety of proteins. Here, they were shown to contain a distinctive composition of RNAs including microRNAs, suggesting that the RNAs are being selectively packaged into them. Furthermore, exosomes could be taken up by other cells, and the microRNAs could have functional effects within the target cells. Thus, exosomes appeared to be a new type of cell-cell communication pathway in the body. Furthermore, a French scientist, Rémy Sadoul, had shown that exosomes are secreted from cultured neurons and their secretion is increased when the neurons are treated with NMDA, which mimics the effects of synaptic stimulation by glutamate, a natural excitatory neurotransmitter.

I became excited by this and contacted the senior author of the *Nature Cell Biology* paper, Jan Lottvall. As it happened, he was visiting another exosome laboratory at the Pasteur Institute in Paris when I was in Paris too, so I came for a visit. He greeted me and the first thing he said was, "Where are you from?" I said, America. He pressed, "No, where are you *really* from?" You have to realize that I had a good tan and am naturally swarthy anyway, and xenophobic Parisians had been approaching me on the street (not in a friendly way) asking if I was from Iraq. So I understood why he was asking. I terminated our interview before it had begun.

I did visit an old colleague who I knew from my retino-tectal days in Einstein, who had become one of France's premier public intellectuals and who had a laboratory at the Pasteur Institute too. He introduced me to his mistress (a sweet postdoc at the Institute) and made sure that I was impressed by his latest papers in *Nature* and *Neuron*, his start-up company to develop a brilliant new product he had developed (it truly was brilliant), his latest neuroscientific philosophy book for the lay public, and his latest play which was being produced in Paris, again, an intelligent mix of philosophy and public affairs. I was quite depressed by this display, not because I was jealous, but because I was sad that such an accomplished, driven man needed to impress me. This one-upmanship is very common at least in certain areas of science: Once I was on a plane to an RNA conference and sat between two well-known scientists, who spent the entire flight talking over me, trying to top the other with stories of their accomplishments. I sat between them quietly, reading papers in their field, entirely un-noticed.

One more story from the Pasteur Institute. I toured the lab of the world's expert on exosomes and was disgusted by another quirk that scientists often display: As I was introduced to various postdocs and staff scientists, their first question to me was: "What have you done in the field of exosomes?" I said, "Nothing at all." They never asked me what I *have* done in any other field, for of course, exosomes were the extent of their interests and world-view! Their scientific view of exosomes was also overly narrow in my opinion. They had studied one kind of exosomes which was generated by one kind of cellular mechanism in a few kinds of cells, and assumed that this could be generalized to all exosomes – nay, that exosomes were in fact defined in terms of how they were generated at the cellular level. I suspected then, and the field knows now, that in fact, there are various kinds of exosomes and they can be generated in several ways.

This is more than a pet-peeve of mine, because I mentioned that I had juxtaposed two threads of science in my hypothesis of exosomes. The first was the study showing that exosomes contain RNAs. The second, however, had to do with electron microscopic studies of synapses in the brain. Little so-called spinules, "little spines" or protrusions are created largely, though not exclusively, at the postsynaptic face of synapses when they are strongly excited, and protrude into the presynaptic face of the synapse where they can be pinched off within the presynaptic neuron. I realized that these "little spines" had many cellular features of budding exosomes, and wrote a paper proposing that they are actually exosomes which are transferring RNAs and proteins from the postsynaptic neuron to its presynaptic partners, during periods of intense activity. As you may imagine, this excited the imagination of neuroscientists, but the exosome biologists were not moved, because these "thorns" were not generated in the same part of the cell as traditional exosomes, nor were they freely secreted, etc.

I attempted to test this hypothesis and wrote several grant proposals to NIH, but they were all triaged (meaning, not discussed or considered for funding). Nevertheless, other examples of exosomal release and transfer of proteins and RNAs have been shown in the nervous system as well as other tissues, and an entire field has sprung up to study exosomes and other extracellular vesicles. I was proud that I contributed a review on synaptic RNAs in the nervous system to a special issue published by *Proceedings of the Royal Society (London)*, which is tied as being the oldest scholarly journal in the world, and certainly one of the most prestigious.

4. Studies of microRNA changes in various learning-related paradigms in mice and rats.

Besides the sort-of-theoretical bioinformatics studies with Vetle, and the mechanistic wet-lab studies with Giovanni, I did a series of collaborative experimental studies with John Larson and Yogesh Dwivedi in which mice or rats were subjected to some learning situation or stress challenge, and then we examined changes across the entire population of microRNAs that occurred in the hippocampus and/or cortex, i.e., regions involved in learning and memory. Our focus was on entire co-regulated modules of miRNAs going up or down in parallel, or indeed the entire population of all miRNAs going up or down. This was in contrast to most neuroscientists who tried to fit miRNAs into a one miRNA – one target paradigm, and chose to examine only one miRNA at a time and its effect on one or a few of its potential targets. Again, I thought that this was premature, a matter of the scientist trying to fit miRNAs into his or her own mindset, rather than looking at a distance and seeing what patterns emerge.

John is an interesting guy; he had arrived at UIC soon after I did, but was placed on the tenure track. He was a student and protégé of Gary Lynch, a flamboyant neuroscientist best known for developing studies of long-term potentiation (LTP), a cellular model of learning and memory. John had shown that a certain type of brain stimulation at so-called theta frequencies greatly enhanced the development of LTP; since theta rhythm is normally generated in the brain during exploration, this was actually a breakthrough both in terms of insight into how learning was encoded in the brain, and as an experimental tool to study LTP. Lynch was at U of California at Irvine, and John had lived in a beach house on Balboa Island off Newport Beach. John was presumably hired as the electrophysiologist for the Costa group, but the reason he came to Chicago is probably because he is an insane fan of the Cubs. He moved across from Wrigley Field so he would be able to watch the games from the roof. John, like so many of his/my generation, was idealistic and philosophical at heart – his goal was not simply to generate findings but to make insights about how the brain actually works (spoiler alert: we still have little idea!).

John, Yogesh and I did find a lot of interesting results, and neuroscientists did pay some attention to them. For example, mice who learned to discriminate between two different odors (olfactory conditioning) showed up-regulation of miRNAs. Rats subjected to repeated foot shock stress showed a difference between those rats which responded to this stress by acting helpless in a swim test (so-called learned helplessness, an animal model of PTSD and depression). The resilient rats showed a big down-regulation of twelve miRNAs whereas those who showed helplessness did not show any changes.

Yogesh and I followed this up by pretreating the rats with enoxacin, an antibiotic which others had shown causes a large overall increase in miRNA levels in tissues including brain. Enoxacin completely prevented the rats from showing learned helplessness, establishing it as a potential treatment for PTSD or depression (or indeed, any other disease that might be associated with a decrease in miRNA production). Enoxacin was already being actively tested as a potential cancer treatment, but this was the first indication that it might have value for neurological or psychiatric diseases. UIC actually filed a provisional use patent application for enoxacin on our behalf, but finalizing the patent required follow-up that Yogesh did not do (he had moved to U of Alabama by this point). Although enoxacin itself is not an ideal drug since it can rarely cause seizures in susceptible individuals, other related drugs have the same efficacy on miRNAs without the effect on seizure thresholds. I attempted to get some funding from several private foundations to evaluate enoxacin further, but was not able to catch their interest in the light of a slew of other repurposed drugs that they were evaluating already.

5. We did three studies of microRNAs in human diseases:

a) We found that microRNA expression is down-regulated and reorganized in prefrontal cortex of depressed suicide subjects.

b) We measured miRNA levels in postmortem pieces of prefrontal cortex from the Stanley Foundation collection which consisted of individuals with schizophrenia, depression, bipolar disease, and matched controls. The most interesting finding was that synaptically-enriched miRNAs were selectively decreased in schizophrenia. This is probably not due to a decreased density of synapses in this disease, since equal amounts of RNA were assayed from synaptosomes prepared from each person. This finding also suggests that enoxacin might help improve schizophrenia by increasing miRNA levels at the synapse.

b) At this time (roughly 2010), I had written seven grant proposals in one year. The only one that I got was a project from the Alzheimer's Association to measure miRNA levels in the blood of individuals with Alzheimer disease (AD) vs. matched controls. Actually, not in the blood per se, but in the small vesicles that we just discussed called exosomes, which circulate in the blood. Although circulating exosomes may arise from many different tissues, and although Alzheimer disease may affect tissues other than brain, I had hoped that we might detect changes in brain-enriched miRNAs which might arise from neurons. Eventually, if we found interesting changes, we could try to purify neural exosomes from the blood using specific antibodies, and magnify the changes in that manner.

The experimental design that we had proposed was *prospective*, and potentially very powerful to see if exosomal miRNAs, singly or in combination, could be biomarkers for people at risk of or in the process of coming down with Alzheimer disease. However, in order for their precious funds to go further, the Alzheimer's Association folks slashed our budget to the extent that we could only do a small *retrospective* study, that is, to see if people already diagnosed with the disease show any miRNA changes compared to controls matched for age, gender and geography. This is much less powerful since any changes that we observed might be the result of the disease, not a predictor of its onset. The study was done in collaboration with the Rush Alzheimer Disease Center, a very large, very efficient operation located just a few blocks down the street from my office at UIC.

We did find some interesting miRNA changes that were associated with Alzheimer disease, and others are following up these findings using neural exosomes in prospective studies. The last few samples were processed by Giovanni during his last day working with me, right before he began a postdoctoral fellowship to study miRNAs in prostate cancer. (Eventually he was offered a tenure track assistant professorship in Pathology, but by that time he had burnt out on academia and took a much better paying job working for a pharmaceutical company.)

I could have continued to measure miRNAs in animals and humans and probably could have continued to get mainstream grants on these topics. However, after Giovanni left, I closed my wet-lab rather than attempt to recruit and train a new person. In part, the field had mushroomed and so I did not feel that I was "needed" in this area. In part, I was discouraged that all my truly novel ideas (siRNAs, exosomes, enoxacin) were unfundable, at least by me. I had been able to get multiple small grants, both from NIH and private foundations, but never obtained the gold-standard R01 grant for any neuroscience project. In part, I could busy myself with informatics, where I was much better appreciated. In part, I was skeptical of findings in the miRNA field, where there was a lack of standardization with blood components and preparation schemes, and no robustness in the published results – every group seemingly finds a rather different set of miRNA changes for comparable experiments. Although I had been proud of running a wet-lab, and my identity had always been as a bench neuroscientist, I closed the second floor lab without looking back. I do have occasional nightmares about my laboratory failures, lack of progress, and lost opportunities, but hey, everyone has nightmares, am I right?

6. siRNAs rise from the dead.

More than a decade after we proposed the existence of siRNAs formed during learning in the mammalian brain, the technology for measuring siRNAs had greatly improved. We took the RNA samples from our mouse hippocampal olfactory discrimination study, and were able to show that siRNAs were detectable and were increased during early stages of learning. Moreover, they were only found in 8 genes, each of which is involved in learning.

Perhaps surprisingly, this provocative finding has not been followed up, to my knowledge, by anyone in mammalian brain. Why not? It would be easy to say that these ideas are still ahead of their time; or perhaps neuroscientists have simply not yet finished mining the effects of miRNAs. Another possible reason is that soon after I published my positive results, a well-known lab published rather similar experiments that found *negative* results – they failed to find siRNAs! This is probably due to the way that they filtered out RNAs expressed at low abundance.

According to Ow and Hall, "the existence of endo-siRNAs in the mammalian nervous system is uncertain and largely unexplored despite the presence of the RNAi machinery in mammalian neurons, which shares some of the same components as the endo-siRNA pathway. This may be in part due to the pervasive belief that siRNAs are primarily silencers of transposons and foreign genetic invaders and not regulators of endogenous genes per se. In addition, assigning a small RNA as a bona fide siRNA, which is a DICER-dependent product derived from dsRNA, has proven difficult." (Ow MC, Hall SE. piRNAs and endo-siRNAs: Small molecules with large roles in the nervous system. Neurochem Int. 2021 May 31;148:105086. doi: 10.1016/j.neuint.2021.105086). I don't expect the field to accept RNA interference already as a means of regulating learning, but given that my studies were conclusively positive and showed highly specific patterns, at least this should encourage others to investigate the area in more detail! Having decided to close my wet-lab, I had also decided not to continue beating my head against the wall trying to pursue such ideas.

Chapter Nine. UIC part 3: Promotion and tenure

Soon after I was promoted to Assistant Professor on the tenure track, I was assigned a faculty mentor. I was lucky enough to be assigned to the vice president for academic affairs, Meena Rao, a physiologist herself. We had only one meeting, in which she told me bluntly that I might not have a future since I don't have the affect of a professor! Maybe Murray Bornstein had not confused me with Steve Baer back at Einstein after all.

Well, not having the affect of a successful faculty member has one huge advantage in academia – being un-noticed means that you are not roped into an endless array of departmental committees, college-level committees, and university-wide committees. This saved me enormous amounts of time that could be spent doing research. Having no talent for administration, I never got the itch to get on the executive track and run a department or program myself, although I did try to get NIH funding to create a few research centers (unsuccessfully) over the years.

It would be nice to say that I had learned from the mistakes that I had made at U of Chicago, and was intent on doing things right the second time to attain promotion and tenure at UIC. However, I think it was more a matter of accepting my flaws and harnessing them, rather than overcoming them to become an ideal academic. For example, I was "lucky" that my appointment was in Psychiatry, a clinical department with no PhD program, which meant that my teaching responsibilities were minimal – although it also meant that I was held responsible for supporting 85% of my efforts through my own external grants. Believe it or not, I write grants better than I teach.

Mini-primer on promotion and tenure. The rules regarding promotion and tenure vary according to the department, the discipline, and even the individual being considered. However, in general, the rising academic is expected to accomplish significant work in three dimensions: *Funded research* (the number and size of grants obtained, and the number and impact of papers published; arguably the most important aspects of the promotion package), *teaching* (including evaluations both from peers and from students), and *service* (e.g., serving on committees and taking leadership roles both within the University and in your chosen discipline). Letters of recommendation are solicited from big names, preferably professors who do not know you personally, but only your work. One is up for tenure after about 7 years but it takes 2-3 years to prepare the package. If not approved, it is up-or-out.

Recall that I was lacking in all three dimensions when I went up for tenure at U of Chicago. I am not sure that I was any less pig-headed at UIC, but I did aim to cover the bases on all three fronts.

As for funded research, I had been Principal Investigator on 8 neuroscience grants after 2000, but this was a double-edged sword since none were R01 grants from

NIH. The R01 grants that I had gotten for informatics saved me.

As for publications, the number, quality, and impact of my research was fine, and Debbie Rissing, the departmental coordinator who enthusiastically helped me put together my tenure package, said that my letters of recommendation were "bulletproof". Right after my promotion went through, she got married and moved to Bolivia to do missionary work. Coincidence?

As for teaching, I had done the required departmental teaching of residents, had assisted in teaching others' neuroscience courses to graduate students, and had given a seminar on Biology of MicroRNAs. Given that my teaching requirements were minimal, this was plenty.

As for service, I did sit on a few University-wide committees, but focused my attention almost solely on service to the neuroscience and informatics professional organizations. The leading neuroscience organization is called the Society for Neuroscience, and although I did give a lecture in one of their short courses and served on their Neuroinformatics committee for one year (before it was abolished), I was never fully embraced by this group, which is probably not unrelated to the fact that the leaders of SfN are also the mainstream orthodoxy who tend to review the R01 neuroscience grants!

Fortunately, the International Society for Neurochemistry was much more amenable to my proposals, and I organized a number of panels, workshops and symposia for them. It was a running joke that disaster accompanied my presentations, for one conference in Hong Kong was postponed for two years due to the SARS epidemic, and another in Cancun was canceled due to a Category V hurricane! I also gave some invited talks on my RNA studies, although most of my invited talks and keynote talks were on literature based discovery, for informatics conferences.

Another aspect of service is taking on leadership roles and I was elected to lead two different SIGs (special interest groups), one on Medical Ethics and one on Knowledge Discovery and Data Management, in what has become my home organization, the American Medical Informatics Association (AMIA). I like AMIA because they are homey yet professional, in contrast to the experiences I had doing similar roles for the American Society for Information Science and Technology (ASIST) (homey but not professional) and the Association for Computing Machinery (ACM) (professional but not homey). I also did considerable service to review grants for NIH, National Science Foundation, and many other public and private foundations around the world.

However, there was one important bellwether of prestige that I had not attained: I had not been invited to serve as an editorial board member for any scholarly journal. I decided to found my own journal so that I would have "Editor in Chief" on my CV. This was not entirely a cynical move at the time, since my journal would cover interdisciplinary topics and articles that did not fit easily into existing journals, specifically, studies of scientific practice, literature based discovery, and tool building. It took about two years to create the journal and convince Biomed Central, a leading open access publisher, to host it. Soon after it appeared, the mega-journal *Plos One* was launched and its wide scope made my journal unnecessary. My journal is called *DISCO: Journal of Biomedical Discovery and Collaboration* and it is still on the books today – anyone can submit an article, have it peer reviewed, and if it is good enough, it will be published online (and archived at PubMed Central) at no cost to the author. However, after I got tenure, I stopped actively soliciting articles for the journal, and it remains in hibernation.

People refer to DISCO as a failure, yet I regard it as having been a resounding success. I am not sure whether founding DISCO did the trick or not, but not long afterwards, I was invited to join the editorial boards of (now) fifteen journals; most are informatics journals but some are in psychiatry or neuroscience, and the list includes the two big mega-journals *Plos One* (where I am Section Editor) and *Scientific Reports*. I am Associate editor for several journals, including one sponsored by AMIA, and have been asked to assist in launching several new journals, so this aspect of service was now more than adequately covered.

Having a MD degree made me popular among computer scientists, who needed someone with medical credibility to help organize conferences on biomedical informatics. In 2010, I assisted in creating a new major conference,

ICHI (International Conference on Healthcare Informatics), which was originally sponsored by ACM but moved to IEEE (the leading organization for engineers) after internal drama between the organizers and the parent organizations. I mention this because I invited the eminent (late) Milton Corn as the inaugural keynote speaker. Milt was a pioneer of information science, an old school bow tie-wearing gentleman, a visionary, who was then in charge of extramural NIH funding at the National Library of Medicine, i.e., the person who set the agenda for who and what will get funded in terms of grants. I mention this because not long after, when Aaron Cohen and I submitted a R01 proposal on evidence based medicine, it was funded even though it did not get a great score. In fact, we were told initially that it would not be funded, and we should prepare a revision, but before the revision could be reviewed, they funded the original proposal -- because it was a priority research area and qualified for Obama stimulus funds. I mention this because Milt Corn was truly the right person of the right stature to open the ICHI conference, and I had not had any cynical motives in extending the invitation. But I do wonder if Milt had a soft spot for me because I had invited him.

As you heard in a previous chapter, Costa never nominated me for promotion, but Flaherty did so anyway. The department voted unanimously in my favor, and over the coming months, my package moved slowly through the College, the University, the Provost and the Board of Regents. Finally, in 2008, I was awarded the title of Associate Professor with Tenure.

Chapter Ten. Post-Arrowsmith informatics

The Arrowsmith project was a blazing success. The Arrowsmith two-node search interface has been up and running as a free, public web service for the past twenty years. We also generated a slew of new models, tools and datasets including ADAM, a database of abbreviations in the biomedical literature; Anne O'Tate, a search engine that takes the results of a PubMed search and processes biomedical literature further in ways that could not otherwise be easily performed; and Author-ity, a large-scale statistical model which predicts, for every article in the biomedical literature, which individuals were authors on that paper. I say individuals, not names, for there are hundreds of different people named John Smith. We predicted the existence of these hundreds of individuals and assigned each of them which articles we believed that they wrote, without reference to any external list (e.g. a census).

We decided to pursue Author-ity further, but to our surprise, the biomedical community did not seem to appreciate the importance of knowing who-wrote-what. We wrote one grant which got scathing reviews from a NIH study section that was *not* run by the National Library of Medicine: They denied the existence of the problem altogether, for surely one could simply assign an ID number to each person on Earth and attach that to each article? (Yes, that could be easily done; why not tattoo that ID number on each person's arm? And why not do it out on Highway 61?)

I also asked to see David Lipman, the head of NCBI, the agency within NIH that maintains all of the scientific databases, including PubMed, the public search engine that retrieves the biomedical literature. He did not see the importance of the problem either, but agreed that he would study the issue. Later he found that one in six searches were for author names, and so yes, this was a significant problem. We wrote another grant proposal, this time to a study section run by the National Library of Medicine, and they gave us a 2 year grant to create and evaluate the Author-ity dataset. Eventually, PubMed implemented their own version of the Author-ity model within their search engine.

Turns out our model was amazingly accurate, and perhaps even more surprising, it turns out that the main audience interested in our work consisted of economists, who were studying innovation, and policy analysts, who wanted to track the careers of funded individuals over time. An economist from Harvard wanted to apply our methods to disambiguate the individuals who obtained U.S. patents, and wanted Vetle and me to collaborate in this project. However, the guy would agree to do things one way, then four days later say that his administrators wanted it done a different way. He had originally asked me to be the Principal Investigator (which he should have done but was too busy or lazy to take on) yet expressed worry that he was not getting enough credit. I ran quickly from this potential collaboration. The upshot was that Vetle became PI and this became his first funded independent grant. A win-win-win.

Soon after, an economist from Ohio State, Bruce Weinberg, invited us to update and improve Author-ity as part of a big economics program project. We have now participated in this for the past six years and hope to renew it. Vetle has built his career largely on creating sophisticated tools that extend Author-ity, for example, a tool that predicts the gender of an individual from their name, and another that predicts their ethnicity. His two kids both have Norwegian names, by the way. He has also linked an individual's articles to their grants, patents, dissertations, cities in which they work, and so on, forming an extremely valuable dataset for scholars to study.

Systematic reviews and evidence based medicine

Although I owe my reputation to having developed literature-based discovery as a collaborator of Don Swanson, I did not have much interest in acting as the big honcho in this emerging field, or trying to anticipate new directions of research. In fact, I was not very happy with the way that LBD had become conceptualized, which is as a link prediction problem: Imagine different ideas or concepts as nodes in a graph, and if they have been mentioned or studied together, connect the nodes by a link. Then LBD can be thought of as predicting which new links are likely to form in the near future. There is nothing wrong with this approach, but I knew from my own LBD insights that most situations don't lend themselves to this formulation. Also, the most likely new links are also the *least* surprising, so this is not a way to find new breakthroughs. I have continued to explore several new avenues in LBD that I will discuss later, but from creating Author-ity I had gotten the taste for doing text mining and statistical modeling that would create useful tools that stimulate discovery more indirectly -- by enabling biologists and other scientists to handle information more efficiently.

Indeed, working in biomedical informatics is nothing like working in neuroscience. The scientific problems are of an entirely different order. For example, one issue in informatics may be to find an appropriate way to compare different journals. There are roughly 5,000 journals in the biomedical literature, and there are many situations in which one would like to ask: given a journal, which journals are most similar to it? Well, one can ask which journals have articles that discuss the most similar topics; or one can ask which journals share the highest percentage of authors who publish articles in both; or one can ask which journals cite each other's articles the most; and so on. These are all related but not identical types of similarity, and different metrics may be better for different research purposes. One also wants to put the value that describes the similarity onto a quantitative scale: but should similarity be expressed as a number between 0 and 1? Between 0 and 100? Or might similarity be given by any positive number going potentially up to infinity? Certainly, similarity does not reflect a linear relationship, since given one journal, a few journals are very similar to it, whereas almost all others show very little similarity. So, creating similarity metrics for journals is not something you discover in nature, but something you craft, like a fine wine. Once the metrics are created and posted as public datasets, a research infrastructure is provided that others can use.

Facilitating the sharing of data, standardizing research resources so they can be reused, ensuring a free flow of information -- these are not simply lip service but in fact drive much of the research in this field, in stark contrast to the dog-eat-dog experience I saw in neuroscience.

In 2008, in the post-Arrowsmith period, I decided to look around to see what other important goals in informatics might not have been adequately studied. After discussions with John Davis and others, I decided that automating the process of writing systematic reviews might be ripe for study using text mining methods and statistical modeling. The best guy in this area was Aaron Cohen, an associate professor in Oregon Health Science University in Portland. Aaron was a protégé of Bill Hersh, one of the founders of biomedical informatics who specialized in information retrieval. Bill was an early friend of literature-based discovery and had helped me found DISCO a few years earlier. We formed a team that included several experts on writing systematic reviews, and began to create a research project.

What exactly are systematic reviews, evidence synthesis, and evidence based medicine? Well, evidence based medicine is the (surprisingly controversial) notion that doctors should base their medical decisions on the existing research, primarily on the peer-reviewed published literature, and preferentially on high-quality evidence such as randomized placebo-controlled trials in contrast to, say, individual case reports. Believe it or not, doctors generally base their medical decisions on their own personal experiences, the prevailing standards of practice of the time (remember leeches and blood-letting?), and clinical guidelines issued by agencies, which may or may not be evidence based. There are three problems with evidence based medicine, however: First, many questions in medicine have no solid research consensus. Second, each individual patient has their own personal circumstances of age, geography, comorbid diseases, genetics, and so forth. A medication that works best in a clinical trial may not necessarily work at all in that individual. Third, it is no easy task to determine if a question in medicine has a solid research consensus or not, and if so, what that consensus is! That involves a process of "evidence synthesis", that is, accumulating all of the relevant evidence and putting it together to try and make sense of it.

The "highest" form of evidence synthesis is the systematic review, which attempts to collect ALL relevant evidence from all sources, published and unpublished, attempts to assess their quality, and often attempts to combine or pool evidence across individual studies (so-called meta-analysis). This is generally done by a team, by hand, and it can take between six months and several years to complete and publish. An initial sweep of the published literature is made, usually consisting of thousands of articles, which are triaged by reading the titles and abstracts, to make a relatively small pile of candidate articles (maybe a few hundred) to be read in their entirety. Finally, an even smaller pile of articles are selected for inclusion in their analysis (maybe a few dozen or even maybe only a few, if any). Additional candidate articles may be found by other means, such as looking at studies that were cited by the included articles, or articles associated with clinical trials that are relevant to the question.

Many systematic reviews find that the evidence base is inadequate to make any conclusion at all, or the conclusions are mixed or of low quality. Systematic reviews can be somewhat subjective as well, since different teams have different ideas of what scope of evidence to consider. Only articles in English? Only articles published recently? Only clinical trials? Slight changes in how the questions are formulated can also affect the evidence that is included in the analysis, and the overall conclusions reached. Nevertheless, systematic reviews are the bedrock of evidence based medicine. We wanted to help systematic review teams write their reviews faster and better, and help them update existing reviews when new evidence appears. It would seem to be a no-brainer that doing all the work by hand is untenable and probably un-necessary. There are two major processes involved in writing a systematic review: a) Finding the relevant articles, and b) extracting data from the included articles and combining the data across studies. We decided to focus on developing automated methods to help them retrieve and triage articles published in the biomedical literature.

As mentioned earlier, Aaron and I were lucky enough to get our R01 proposal funded on our first submission (though after 14 months delay!) and we began a collaboration that continues to this day. We renewed the grant once, making ten years of working together so far, and have succeeded in creating a neat suite of tools that are broadly valuable for biologists, medical researchers, and the informatics community, as well as the systematic review teams that we originally targeted.

We had one big flame-out failure – a web tool called Metta, which allowed a user to enter a single query that was sent to five different biomedical databases of articles, and then retrieve them, removing duplicate articles along the way. The problem was not that the tool failed to work, but it required constant maintenance by individuals, which is not feasible for an academic project that lacks the resources of a commercial web team. Whenever one of the five databases made any un-announced change on their end, we needed to detect that somehow and make a change on our end so that the results would be correct. After working on this for seven years, and failing to find a commercial vendor who wanted to take it over, we finally pulled the plug.

We also faced unexpected resistance from the systematic review community to our automation efforts. They do not want to lose even 1% of the relevant articles, even if they save 70% of their overall effort. We initially tried to create a seamless pipeline of tools that would feed from one automatically to the other, but each systematic review team has their own ways of working and their own individual requirements, so the pipeline idea was abandoned after a few years too.

But to focus on the positives, we did create a long list of models and practical tools that were beautiful and broadly valuable for the systematic review community and beyond. I will only mention them briefly:

- We devised "RCT Tagger" and "Human Tagger" to automatically predict if a given article is a randomized controlled trial, or human-related; eventually we created "Multi-tagger" to predict 50 of the most important publication types and study designs! These taggers help discard irrelevant articles during systematic review triage and so can reduce effort significantly.
- "Aggregator" takes a list of randomized controlled trial articles, and predicts which articles are likely to arise from the same underlying clinical trial. Seven articles from one trial don't count as much as seven articles from seven trials.
- "Deduplicator" takes several lists of articles from different databases and removes the duplicates to create a single merged list.
- "Trials to Publications" allows the user to select any given clinical trial registered in ClinicalTrials.gov, and predicts which articles are likely to present clinical outcome data from that trial.
- "Citation Cloud" allows the user to select any article, and visualize the list of articles cited by that article; the list of articles that cite it; and

those that are co-cited and bibliographically coupled to it (I won't explain this jargon, but they are different ways of identifying related articles.)

- "Anne O'Tate" takes the results of a PubMed search engine query, and processes it further in all sorts of cool ways.
- We also created a variety of basic text resources for further text processing purposes, such as similarity metrics for journals, medical topics, and terms (words and phrases), and devised a new way of representing words and phrases as vectors, which are disseminated publicly for others to use.

Promotion to full professor

I waited a full eight years to go up for promotion to full professor, and took another two years for the promotion to be approved. Why wait? For one thing, the increase in salary is pretty trivial ($2,000 per year in base salary). For another, the timing has to be right, so I waited until our R01 grant had been renewed. Unlike the angst and machinations involved in the tenure decision earlier, I don't remember any major issues involved in becoming full professor. Besides demonstrating sustained scholarship (continued grants and continued publishing of articles), I hit two milestones that counted: First, I was invited to be a standing member of a NIH Study Section -- in biomedical informatics. (What discipline did you think it was in? Are you even *skimming* this book?) Second, I wrote a textbook.

The textbook story is worth telling. Once I had closed my wet-lab, I became increasingly aware of how badly designed many neuroscience experiments are. Actually, the problem is pervasive in biomedical research, not just neuroscience, and statisticians had been writing about this for years, documenting with mathematical precision just how unreliable are the findings reported in biomedical articles. Yet changing current scientific practice is a huge uphill battle, since the incentives are almost entirely in favor of the status quo.

I felt this resistance myself, as I volunteered to teach a course in "Data Literacy" for neuroscience graduate students. The idea was to give students an intuitive feel for the statistical issues involved in designing experiments, rather than to have them memorize formulas. Yet as I lectured the students on what is, and what is not, acceptable scientific practice, I found that I was contradicting what their own advisors had been telling them to do for their thesis studies. Who was I to tell eminent professors that they were publishing flawed studies? Well, I stopped giving this course, took my lecture notes, and wrote them into a textbook, "Data Literacy", which was accepted by a major publisher, Elsevier. The most fun part of creating the book was collaborating with a young artist, Stephanie Muscat, who had gotten a bachelor's degree in neuroscience and was completing a master's at the Rhode Island School of Design. She and I brainstormed the illustrations which were both whimsical and scientifically informative.

After writing the textbook, I did one scholarly study of experimental design, working with statistics students at UIC, showing that the number of mice routinely used in a popular preclinical assay for antidepressant actions is far short of the number needed for reliable results, despite the fact that the assay does produce large, nay huge effects.

The fact that I have taken time to write this book should tell you that I am at a crossroads, trying to decide how to move forward scientifically. Yes, there is plenty of interesting research to do in informatics, and I might have the energy to tackle the subject of improving experimental design if I feel scrappy. But probably the most intriguing set of issues that I see are related to literature based discovery.

Classic LBD seeks to identify entirely new, previously unformulated or at least unstudied hypotheses. However, I am currently interested in finding ways to identify ideas and findings that were previously raised but were abandoned, neglected, experimentally refuted, led to dead ends, or were simply not taken seriously. Some of these are simply wrong-headed research directions, of course, but some may have simply been ahead of their time, and abandoned because the methods of the time were not adequate to test them or because the concepts of the time could not encompass them. These are critical places where reassessing the old findings in light of newer studies might create new scientific paradigms. My next book will be called, "I have Abandoned the Search for Truth and am Looking for a Good Fantasy"!

Coda

Formulating a hypothesis is like writing a song. Any schlub can do it, and there is an entire journal called *Medical Hypotheses* to prove it. Formulating a *fertile* hypothesis, on the other hand, is as deceptively difficult as writing a *good* song, and I have gained recognition as someone adept at this art. Indeed, Don Swanson and I created an entirely new scientific genre of literature-based discovery analyses which, as I have shown, motivated many of my hypotheses and laboratory findings which, in turn, have prefigured entire fields of study in neuroscience and genomics.

Yet even today, when I see one of the mainstream neuroscientists, at seminars, conferences, or just passing them in the halls of UIC, I see a patronizing look on their faces, sometimes accompanied by a withering comment. One colleague in my department who I had worked with all through the Costa days said, "I did not know you were still here." To them, I am a failure who never got established and eventually closed his lab. I used to have a joint appointment in a basic science department, Anatomy and Cell Biology, a hold-over from the days when George Pappas was chairman and I taught and collaborated with faculty members there. I would have had to get a letter of recommendation from the new chairman at the time that I was going up for full professor – I wrote him asking if there was any need for my services and he did not bother even to reply.

They say the best revenge is living well. Dr. Costa is commemorated today by a half-page entry in Wikipedia. Tom Jessell, who held court at Columbia for decades, was sacked for not following the rules on sexual conduct and died of a progressive neurological disease soon thereafter. James Watson, whose memoir "The Double Helix" was as brilliant as his scientific studies on DNA and his administration of Cold Spring Harbor Laboratory, was also sacked for running his mouth with brain out of gear and has been laying low. Me? I have 29 vacation days that I need to take before August 15th or else I lose them.

Chapter Eleven. Reflections on practicing science

<u>Never hired</u>

One of the unusual aspects of my career is that I never obtained a faculty position in the usual way, i.e., by reading an ad that describes the necessary qualifications, applying for it, going through a series of interviews, and negotiating with the chairman about salary, start-up funds, and space. It is not quite true that I never applied for a job in this manner – I did once interview at U of Florida in Gainesville for a neuroscience faculty position before I went to UIC. The steam bath that was Gainesville in summer was not the problem, and I had great respect for the neuroscientists that met with me. One of them kindly and carefully pointed out that I had not yet formulated a realistic (read: fundable) research project and was basically floundering at that point.

The two times that I did obtain a position, there was no opening and no ad. At U of C, I simply found a sponsor, Nancy Schwartz, who was willing to host me if I could find my own funding, and with that foot in the door, I eventually slid my entire body in. At UIC, I found a mentor, Erminio Costa, who was also willing to host me and let me find my way as long as I fit into his own agenda.

Would I do this again? Given my lack of interview skills, this was probably a good strategy in the short term, since I probably could not, and even still cannot, make a good impression in an interview. I also avoided extensive teaching commitments. In the long term, not being hired means that the university had nothing invested in me. I did not fit into their strategic plans, I did not fill any need, and I was not part of any larger programs. It was "easy come, easy go" on their part. So, to the extent that I would deign to give advice to a young academic, I would say to consider creating your own position only if you are committed to your own research and prefer to be independent.

Pursue process or pursue goals?

Charlie the Tuna has good taste, but what the public wants is tuna that tastes good! Similarly, I want to be a great scientist, but what the public wants is scientists who make great discoveries. And making a discovery is something that is largely unpredictable. Entire tomes have been written on factors that influence the chance of making a great discovery, but suffice it to say that they are not entirely under your conscious control or force of will. Intelligence, training, and intuition do not ensure that you will make a discovery, much less a great one.

Therefore, a scientist cannot set "make a great discovery" as a *goal*, or anything else which is not under their direct control (such as winning prizes or achieving immortal fame). Instead, one must follow a *process* or set of processes, which attempt to create conditions that maximize the chances of making discoveries, be they small or great. (And, I suppose one must avoid self-sabotage, actively shunning the opportunity to make a great discovery because it involves going outside one's comfort level.)

John Lennon wrote "Imagine", but he also wrote "Meat City" and covered songs like "Dizzy, Miss Lizzy". Bob Dylan wrote "Blowin' in the Wind" but he also wrote "Bob Dylan's 115th Dream" and covered songs by Frank Sinatra. *Perfectionism* does not describe their creative output as well as *fertility* – they let a thousand flowers bloom, of all sizes and colors. Perhaps it is more appropriate to think of creative output, including scientific discoveries, as your children -- they have their lives, and their own futures; you cannot control or even anticipate how they will turn out. Yet of course parents should attempt to follow a *process* of raising their kids that will maximize the chances that they stay out of jail and have happy, productive lives of their own.

You may have surmised at this point that I don't plan to write down an explicit list of what process or processes I think a budding scientist should follow to become the best scientist that they can be. (Rise early every morning and read for an hour? Make sure to eat lots of fiber? Stan Crain was an enthusiastic proponent of wheat bran; myself, I favor kale.) This not only assumes that I *have* become the best that I can be, it also assumes that anyone else could or should follow in my footsteps. You should read Scott Adams' book "How to Fail at Almost Everything and Still Win Big" to learn more about process vs. goals, and how to choose processes for yourself.

For the moment, my point is simple: Focus on what you can personally control, which is your own planning, efforts and decisions, and don't worry about what you cannot control.

How I run a lab

I actually have a fair number of collaborators and second-hand students – that is, I work with students who are being officially supervised by another professor. In this fashion, the lab is far more horizontally organized than most. I try to approach students not as students per se but as fellow investigators. I do not have two tiers of workers (those who have the ideas and design the experiments vs. those who handle the pipets or who analyze the data and write programs). Instead, I expect everyone to contribute ideas, and everyone to do scut work as needed. I do not try to motivate or excite my students – and many of them leave because the problems do not resonate with them, as indeed they should.

When I interview a prospective student (generally at the graduate or postdoctoral level), I give them a possible problem to tackle, and watch how they think. Do they adapt or recycle ideas from some similar issues they faced in the past? The really good ones will think the problem through from first principles. For undergraduates or prospective technicians, I have learned from experience to ask them to multiply two numbers using paper but no calculator. Over half flame out on this alone.

Programmatic research

There are three features of successful R01 proposals:

- They outline a systematic plan over the entire grant period (usually five years). In other words, they outline a program. In still other words, this *is programmatic research.*
- They phrase the project as tackling a disease (e.g. Alzheimer disease) or a biological function (e.g., learning) rather than simply studying a phenomenon or a molecule.
- They attempt to elucidate mechanisms or test hypotheses rather than to characterize effects per se.

I know this; I have known this since 1983, when I first started writing grants. Yet I have never succeeded in getting a R01 grant in neuroscience, whereas as I keep mentioning, I have gotten three R01 grants to date in informatics. Why? I was applying to both disciplines during the same time period (2000 to 2012) so I did not simply learn how to write grants better over time.

Perhaps the answer is related to the nature of neuroscience itself. Going back to the time of Cajal over a hundred years ago, our progress in understanding the brain has been driven by new methods – the Golgi stain, tissue culture, EEG, the microelectrode, fMRI imaging, calcium imaging, electron microscopy, single-cell gene expression profiling, to name a few. Experimental manipulations used to focus on making small lesions or stimulating small spots in specific brain regions, and now include optogenetic stimulation or inhibition of specific neurons. This emphasis on developing and exploiting new techniques allows neuroscientists to keep very busy and seemingly productive.

In contrast, our theoretical understanding of what the brain does, and how, is very rudimentary. Little progress has been made, and most experiments do not connect closely to theory. Broadly speaking, there are three theories of brain:

- Brain as an electrical machine. Neurons fire action potentials that stimulate or inhibit other neurons in a network. The overall pattern of firing determines what the brain does, but there is a lot of spontaneous activity so that neurons do not simply respond to external inputs.
- Brain as a chemical machine. Neurons change their chemistry, both internally (calcium fluxes and gene expression changes) and externally (release of neurotransmitters and other chemicals that affect other neurons and glial cells). Neurons and glial cells can also grow, change their shape, and change their connections with other cells, as well as multiply and die under certain conditions.
- Brain as a computer (or predictive device). The purpose of the brain is to integrate past and present experiences and information, to predict or anticipate what will happen in the future.

In between methods and theory, there are many puzzling and intriguing phenomena, which are somewhat like orphans because their mechanisms and significance are unclear. To give a few examples, the DNA within neurons (and other cells) can be chemically modified without changing the DNA sequence; this so-called epigenetic regulation provides another layer that controls whether signals can turn the genes on or off. The DNA within neurons can actually show some rearrangements, as small transposable elements move from place to place within chromosomes, disrupting certain genes and possibly altering others. The bulk of DNA within the human genome does not code for proteins, but consists of "junk" DNA sequences (some of which are related to the transposable elements). Neurotransmitters generally are released from presynaptic neurons to their postsynaptic partners, but some chemicals are released in all directions within the brain, and some go upstream from postsynaptic to presynaptic neuron. I already mentioned the possibility of RNA interference in the brain, and the evidence that neurons can communicate by releasing vesicles (or protruding spinules) that carry RNAs and proteins. Relatively few laboratories study such phenomena, and only to the extent that they can piggyback their studies on more mainstream programs. Two orphan phenomena that once were the province of crackpots but hit the mainstream recently are the transgenerational inheritance of acquired characteristics, and the influence of gut bacteria (the so-called microbiome) on human health and disease, but they are rare exceptions to the rule.

My gut feeling (no pun intended) is that the puzzling phenomena are the ones that are most interesting to study, precisely because their mechanisms and significance are unknown. Any well-trained hack can mutate a residue in the phosphorylation site of a dopamine receptor whose function is well characterized and can be directly related to e.g., addiction behavior, which is the kind of research that is best suited to a R01 project. In contrast, my old collaborator Guenter Albrecht-Buehler chose to study whether cells can send infrared light signals to communicate with other cells, a weird phenomenon that he was able to publish in the Proceedings of the National Academy of Sciences but would never, ever get NIH funding (though he did manage to get support from the Air Force Office of Scientific Research at one point).

Throughout the history of neuroscience, new discoveries have found resistance, in part because scientists did not see how they were "necessary" for brain function given existing concepts. Once, there was only one excitatory and one inhibitory neurotransmitter known; it was "un-necessary" to have dozens of such modulatory agents. Once, neurogenesis was "un-necessary" and even incompatible with the accepted idea that the number and connections of neurons are fixed. We have transcription factors to turn genes on and off, so it is "un-necessary" to have epigenetic regulation on top of this. And so on. So, the puzzling orphan phenomena have a psychological value, serving as a reminder and challenge to neuroscientists that their concepts of the brain are woefully incomplete, and possibly misdirected entirely. Only then will experiments have the possibility to shake up brain theories.

Permission to make discoveries?

Another amusing /slash/ irritating aspect of mainstream science is that the esteemed leaders of a field often serve as gate-keepers of accepted knowledge, so that any scientist who reports a discovery has to obtain their permission before the rest of the field is willing to take it seriously. In part, this reflects the relative unreliability of experiments, so that if a person does not make the finding themselves, *de facto* they don't trust other people's surprising research findings no matter how good they may look on paper.

A famous example is the secretion of neurotransmitter via vesicles. Sir Bernard Katz won the Nobel prize for demonstrating vesicular release at the neuromuscular junction, and for years, vigorously fought claims that non-vesicular release occurred instead (or as well). That is, until he demonstrated the existence of non-vesicular release himself.

Another example is neurogenesis in various regions of the adult brain, first shown in the mouse and rat, then in primates and humans. Acceptance of this idea was held back for about twenty years because of opposition by Pasko Rakic at Yale (see Kaplan MS. Environment complexity stimulates visual cortex neurogenesis: death of a dogma and a research career. Trends Neurosci. 2001 Oct;24(10):617-20. doi: 10.1016/s0166-2236(00)01967-6).

True, extraordinary claims require extraordinary evidence, and when there is no mechanism known that can explain the effects, it is natural to be skeptical. In fact, we have a duty to be skeptical. But I worry that there is also the unstated message given to young scientists: If you are a nobody from Nowheresville, you don't have permission to make a significant or surprising discovery. Leave that for the Ivy League and for the Nobel prize winners and their students.

Giving yourself permission is one of those things over which you have complete control.

APPENDIX

Neil R. Smalheiser, MD, PhD
Academic Curriculum Vitae as of June 2021:

Professor with Tenure (8/18- present);
Member, Psychiatric Institute, University of Illinois at
Chicago, 9/96 - present.
Affiliated Faculty, School of Information Sciences
(iSchool), University of Illinois at Urbana-Champaign,
5/18 – present.

Department of Psychiatry, UIC Psychiatric Institute M/C
912
1601 W. Taylor Street, room 525
Chicago, IL 60612
Phone: 312-413-4581;
fax 312-413-4569;
neils@uic.edu.

EDUCATION
Intern, Department of Pediatrics, University of Chicago,
Chicago, IL   1982-1983
Albert Einstein College of Medicine, New York, NY

MD-PhD (Neuroscience) 1982
University of Iowa, Iowa City, IA,

B. A. with Honors (major: mathematics)
1974

PREVIOUS EMPLOYMENT
Research Assistant Professor, Assistant Professor,
Associate Professor (with Tenure)
University of Illinois at Chicago, Chicago, IL.
Department of Psychiatry, 1996-2018.

Postdoctoral Fellow, Instructor, and Assistant Professor
University of Chicago, Chicago, IL, Department of
Pediatrics, 1982-1996.

LICENSURE
Licensed physician, State of Illinois 1983 – present.
CPR – Basic Life Support Certification 7/12.

PROFESSIONAL MEMBERSHIPS
American Medical Informatics Association (Fellow);
Association for Computing Machinery (Senior Member);
Association for Computational Linguistics. Associate,
Behavioral and Brain Sciences; International Brain
Research Organization; International Society for
Neurochemistry; Sigma Xi.

HONORS AND AWARDS
Ford Future Scientists of America Regional Award,
1968.
National Merit Finalist, 1971.
B. P. O. Elks Scholarship, 1971.
Honors Scholarships, University of Iowa, 1971-1973.

Phi Beta Kappa, 1972.
Graduation with Honors and with High Distinction, 1974.
NIH Medical Scientist Training Program Fellowship, 1974-1981.
NIH NRSA individual postdoctoral training award, 1984-1985.
Schweppe Foundation career development award, 1987-1990.
Andrew W. Mellon Foundation Fellow, 1988-1989.
Frontiers Community Support Fund award in recognition for service as an Associate Editor for Frontiers in Digital Humanities, 2017.
Senior Member of ACM, 2018.
Fellow of AMIA, 2020.

COMMITTEE ASSIGNMENTS AND ADMINISTRATIVE SERVICES

Reviewing for NIH Study Sections: (including neuroscience, drug abuse, bio-computing and informatics programs)

- National Library of Medicine Biomedical Informatics Library and Data Science Review Committee, standing member, term July 1, 2017 – June 30, 2021.
- BISTI National Centers for Excellence in Bio-Computing Special Emphasis Panels, 4/01, 9/01, 3/02.
- Neuroinformatics Special Emphasis Panel (Human Brain Project), 9/01, 12/04.

- National Library of Medicine Special Emphasis Panels 3/03, 4/04.
- NIH Molecular Neuroscience Special Emphasis Panel, 8/13.
- Molecular, Cellular, and Developmental Neuroscience Integrated Review Group 7/04.
- NIDA CEBRA Award review 9/04, 3/13, 3/14, 11/14; R21/33 review 5/09.
- Challenge grants 2009.
- NCRR Centers (COBRE and RCMI), 2009.
- National Library of Medicine Technology Review Panel (ARRA contracts), 8/04.
- National Center for Complementary and Alternative Medicine (NCCAM), 2/12, 12/17.
- P41 Centers, 2011, 2019.
- PASC (post-Covid cohort studies), 2021.

Reviewing for other funding agencies:
- National Science Foundation (programs on Developmental & Cellular Neuroscience and Genes & Genome Systems).
- NSF-NIH Panels, 2012, 2015, 2018.
- US Army Medical Research and Materiel Command.
- Department of Health, U. K.
- US-Israel Binational Science Foundation.
- Israel Science Foundation; Basic Science Foundation (Israel Academy of Sciences and Humanities).
- University of Liège, Belgium.

- Alzheimer's Association.
- Autism Speaks.
- Research Grants Council (RGC) of Hong Kong.
- Kentucky Commercialization Fund.
- Netherlands Genomics Initiative (Horizon programme).
- Research Fund "Medizinische Forschungsförderung Innsbruck" of Innsbruck Medical University.
- Parkinson's Disease Society (UK).
- Prinses Beatrix Fonds, The Netherlands.
- India Alliance (Wellcome).
- Medical Research Council (MRC), UK.
- Netherlands Organisation for Scientific Research (NWO).
- Human Frontier Science Program.
- Research Foundation - Flanders (Fonds Wetenschappelijk Onderzoek - Vlaanderen, FWO).
- ICOB (International Collaborations in Organismal Biology), partnership between the NSF and the Israeli Binational Science Foundation.
- Neurological Foundation of New Zealand.
- Agence Nationale de la Recherche, France.
- Austrian Academy of Sciences.
- Prince Center for Neurodegenerative Diseases, Technion, Haifa, Israel.
- NSERC (Natural Sciences and Engineering Research Council of Canada).
- The Croatian Science Foundation (HRZZ).

Leadership positions in National Organizations:
American Medical Informatics Association:
Ethical, Legal & Social Issues Working Group Chair-Elect/Chair/Past Chair 2003-2007.
Knowledge Discovery and Data Mining Working Group Chair-Elect/Chair/Past Chair 2008-2011.
Scientific Program Committee of annual symposium, 2012, 2019.
Working Group Steering Committee, 2018-2019.

Society for Neuroscience:
Neuroinformatics Committee, member, 2009-2010.

Association for Computing Machinery (ACM):
Special Interest Group on Health Informatics (SIGHIT), Vice Chair, 2011-2012.
Member, ACM Health Informatics Task Force, 2011-2013.

American Society for Information Science and Technology (ASIST):
Committee on Communications and Publications, Co-Chair, 2011-2012.
SIG Metrics, Chair-Elect/Chair, 2016-2018.

Organizer or Member of Program Committee for International Conferences:

- The 17th European Conference on Machine Learning and the 10th European Conference on Principles and Practice of Knowledge Discovery in Databases, September 18-22, 2006, Berlin, Germany.

- **BioCreAtIvE** - Critical Assessment for Information Extraction in Biology Conference, April 23-25, 2007, October 7-9, 2009; Madrid, Spain. 2011, TBA.
- Pacific Symposium for Biocomputing, Hawaii, HI, January 4-8, 2008.
- IDAMAP: Intelligent Data Analysis in bioMedicine And Pharmacology, Verona, Italy, 2009; Washington, DC, 2010; Pisa, Italy, 2012.
- ACM 1st International Conference on Health Informatics, Washington, DC, November 11-12, 2010. Program Committee co-Chair for Medicine.
- EFMI (European Federation for Medical Informatics) Special Topic Conference, Lasko, Slovenia, April 14-15, 2011. Paris, France, April 17-19, 2016.
- 7th Conference of the Austrian Computer Society (OCG) Workgroup: Human-Computer Interaction & Usability Engineering (HCI&UE), Graz, Austria. November 25-26, 2011.
- 1st International Conference on Health Information Science, Beijing, China, April 8-10, 2012.
- Medical Informatics Europe (MIE) Conference, Pisa, Italy, August 26-29, 2012. MIE 2014, Istanbul, August 31st - September 3rd, 2014. Madrid, Spain, May 27-29, 2015. Manchester, UK, April 24-27, 2017. Gothenburg April 24-26, 2018.
- HI-BI-BI, International Symposium on Network Enabled Health Informatics, Bio-Medicine and Bioinformatics, Istanbul, Turkey, 27-28 August, 2012. Niagara Falls, 26-27 August, 2013. Beijing,

China, August, 2014. Paris, France, August, 2015. Davis, CA, August 2016.

- Program co-Chair, The First International Workshop on the role of Semantic Web in Literature-Based Discovery, IEEE International Conference on Bioinformatics and Biomedicine (BIBM), Philadelphia, October 4-7, 2012.

- Senior Program Committee, IEEE International Conference on Healthcare Informatics (ICHI), Philadelphia, September 9-11, 2013. Verona, Italy, September 15-17, 2014, ICHI 2015, Dallas, TX, October 21-23, 2015. Local Chair and Senior Program Committee, Chicago, IL, October 4-7, 2016. Senior PC for the Analytics Track, Park City, UT August 1-4, 2017. ICHI 2018 June 27-29 2018 in Heidelberg, Germany. Program Committee Chair in Analytics and Organizer of Embeddings Workshop, ICHI 2019, June 10-13 in Xi'an, China. ICHI 2020, June 15-18 in Oldenburg, Germany (online). ICHI 2021, August 9-12, Victoria, BC.

- Scientific Committee, ACM/IEEE International Conference on Human Factors in Computing & Informatics (SouthCHI 2013), Maribor, Slovenia, July 1-3, 2013.

- Program Committee, International Conference on Brain and Health Informatics (BHI'13), Maebashi, Japan, Oct. 29-31, 2013. Warsaw, Poland, August 2014. BIH '16, Omaha, NB, October 2016.

- Program Committee co-Chair, 3rd International Health Information Science Conference, Shenzhen, China, April 2014.

- International Scientific Committee member, Expert Network HCI-KDD, 2013-present.
- Program Committee, International Society for Computational Biology (ISMB), Boston, MA, July 9-12, 2010. July 11-15, 2014. Dublin, Ireland, July 12-17, 2015. Orlando, FL, July 8-12, 2016.
- Program Committee and Speaker, ACM KDD Workshop on Discovery Informatics, August 24, New York, NY, 2014.
- International Program Committee, Bioinformatics 2015 at BIOSTEC 2015, Lisbon, Portugal, January 12-15, 2015; Rome, Italy, February 21-23, 2016. Porto, Portugal, February 21-23, 2017.
- FORCE2015 organizing committee, co-chair of pre-conference workshops, Portland, OR 2016.
- Program Committee, IEEE IRI-HI 2015, San Francisco, CA, August 13-15, 2015.
- Program Committee, 13th Intl. Congress on Nursing Informatics, Geneva, Switzerland, June 26-29, 2016.
- International Program Committee, International Society for Scientometrics & Informetrics (ISSI2017), to be held in Wuhan, China, 16–20 October 2017.
- Program Committee, International Conference on Brain Informatics (BI'17), Beijing, China, Nov 2017; BI'18, Arlington, TX, Dec 2018; BI '19, Haikou, China, Dec 2019.
- Advisory Board, Next Generation Sequencing & Single Cell Analysis Congress, 2017, Oxford Global Conferences.

- Program Committee, CD-MAKE 2018 (International Cross Domain Conference for Machine Learning & Knowledge Extraction), Hamburg, Germany, August 27-30, 2018.
- Review committee on Information Retrieval, Conference on Empirical Methods in Natural Language Processing and the Intl Joint Conference on Natural Language Processing 2019 (EMNLP-IJCNLP 2019), Hong Kong, November 3–7, 2019.
- Reviewer, AAAI 2020 : The Thirty-Fourth AAAI Conference on Artificial Intelligence, New York, NY Feb 7-12, 2020. AAAI 2021, virtual conference.
- Co-organizer, 1st International Workshop on Literature Based Discovery, co-located with PAKKD, Singapore, May 10, 2020 (held virtually).
- First Workshop on Scholarly Document Processing @ EMNLP 2020 (held virtually).
- First Workshop on Bibliographic Data and Analysis (bibliodap.uni-koblenz.de) to be co-hosted by KDD2021 on August 14-18, 2021 in Singapore.

Membership on Editorial Boards and Advisory Boards:
- *PLOS ONE.* Open access, Public Library of Science. Academic Editor, 2011-present. Section Editor, 2014-present.
- *Frontiers in Research Metrics and Analytics.* Associate Editor, 2015- 2019. Associate Editor, Text Mining and Literature based Discovery specialty section, 2019- present.

- *Journal of Healthcare Informatics Research,* Springer, Associate Editor, 2016-present.
- *JAMIA Open,* Associate Editor, Oxford Academic Press, 2017 – present.
- Founding Editor-in-Chief, *Journal of Biomedical Discovery and Collaboration.* Published by BioMed Central, 2005-2008; hosted by University of Illinois, 2009-present. This peer reviewed, open access journal has the unique goal of bringing together three different groups of researchers in a common forum for the first time: namely, laboratory investigators, informatics researchers who make tools to enhance discovery and collaboration, and social scientists who study scientific practice. The Editorial Board includes internationally known leaders in each of these 3 disciplinary areas, including deans, department chairmen, named professors, program/center directors, and a Nobel laureate.
- *Biology Direct.* Open access, BioMed Central. Editorial board member, 2005- present.
- *Scientific Reports.* Open access, Nature Publishing Group. Editorial board member, in the topic area of psychiatry, 2015-present.
- *Frontiers in Neuroinformatics,* Frontiers Research Foundation. Open access. Editorial board member, 2007- present.
- *Frontiers in Genetics (Non-coding RNA* section), Frontiers, open access, 2014-present.
- *Biomedical Informatics Insights*, Libertas Academica. Open access. 2007-present.

- *Health Information Science and Systems (HISS).* Biomed Central, open access. 2011-present.
- *Network Modeling and Analysis in Health Informatics and Bioinformatics.* Springer, 2012-present.
- *Health Systems*, Palgrave Macmillan, 2011-present.
- *Journal of Data and Information Science*, 2015-present.
- *Journal of Psychiatry and Brain Science,* Qingres, open access, 2016- present.
- *Transactions of the IL State Academy of Science.* Editorial Board member and Chair, Science, Mathematics and Technology Education Division, 1994-1996.
- Member, Technical Advisory Board for "VIVO, Enabling National Networking of Scientists," 2009-2014. This is a NIH-funded multi-institutional consortium (Mike Conlon, Univ. of Florida, PI) that will use Semantic Web-enabled technologies to facilitate querying and collaboration across disciplines and institutions.

Ad Hoc Reviewer:
- *Neuroscience and Psychiatry Journals*: Alzheimer's & Dementia; Behavioral and Brain Functions; Behavioral and Brain Sciences; Biological Psychiatry; Brain Research; Cardiovascular Psychiatry and Neurology; Cellular and Molecular Neurobiology; The Cerebellum; European Journal of Neurology; Frontiers of Neuroscience; Genes, Brain and Behavior;

International Review of Neurobiology; Journal of
Cerebral Blood Flow and Metabolism; Journal of
Neurochemistry; Journal of the Neurological Sciences;
Journal of Neuroscience; Journal of Neuroscience and
Behavioral Health; Journal of Neuroscience Research;
Journal of Psychiatric Research; Molecular Psychiatry;
Nature Reviews Neuroscience; Neuropharmacology;
Neuroreport; Neuroscience; Neuroscience Research;
Restorative Neurology & Neuroscience; Trends in
Neurosciences.

- *Other Biomedical Journals:*

Acta Biotheoretica; Acta Histochemica; American
Journal of Medical Genetics; Biochemical Journal;
Biochemical Pharmacology; Biochimica et Biophysica
Acta (BBA) – Gene Regulatory Mechanisms;
Biochemical Society Transactions; Bioscience Reports;
BMC Developmental Biology; BMC Genomics; BMC
Systems Biology, BMJ Open; Briefings in Functional
Genomics and Proteomics; Cell Research; Cellular &
Molecular Biology Letters; Clinical Science; CNS
Drugs; Exosomes and Microvesicles; Experimental Cell
Research; Hereditas; Human Molecular Genetics;
International Journal of Biochemistry & Cell Biology;
International Journal of Molecular Sciences; IUBMB
Life; Journal of Biological Chemistry; Journal of Cell
Biology; Journal of Clinical Investigation; Journal of
Heredity; Journal of the Royal Society Interface; Life
Sciences; Mechanisms of Aging and Development;
Methods; Mobile Genetic Elements; Molecular Biology
and Evolution; Nature Communications; Nature
Structural and Molecular Biology; Noncoding RNA;
Nucleic Acids Research; Oncogene; Pharmacogenomics

Journal; PLOS Biology; PLOS Computational Biology; Proceedings of the National Academy of Sciences USA; Proceedings of the Society of Experimental Biology and Medicine; RNA; Scientific Data; Trends in Genetics; Trends in Pharmacological Sciences; Wiley Interdisciplinary Reviews: RNA.

- *Informatics and Policy Journals:*
Annual Review of Information Science and Technology; ACI Open (Applied Clinical Informatics); Bioinformatics; BMC Bioinformatics; BMC Medical Informatics and Decision Making; Evidence Based Library and Information Practice; Frontiers in Neuroinformatics; Health Information Science and Systems; IEEE/ACM Transactions on Computational Biology and Bioinformatics; Information Processing & Management; International Journal of Medical Informatics; Journal of the American Medical Informatics Association; Journal of the American Society of Information Science & Technology; Journal of Biomedical Informatics; Journal of Clinical Epidemiology; Journal of Medical Internet Research; Journal of Informetrics; Knowledge Engineering Review; Knowledge and Information Systems; Neuroinformatics; Research Policy; Scientometrics.

- *Multi-Disciplinary and Humanities Journals:*
Applied Economics Letters; Isis; Issues in Integrative Studies; Perspectives in Biology and Medicine; Synthese.

- *Conferences and Books:*
American Medical Informatics Association Annual Symposium; AMIA Informatics Summits; American Society for Information Science and Technology

(ASIST); Conference on Empirical Methods in Natural Language Processing (EMNLP); Medinfo (International Medical Informatics Association); MIE (European Federation for Medical Informatics, EFMI). Blackwell Press (for a book on scientific discovery and one on exosome biology).

Service for NIH Office of Neuroinformatics
Leader of Human Brain Project Working Group on Data Mining, 2005-present.

University of Illinois at Chicago Service Involvement:
- Chair, UIC Faculty Senate Committee on Academic Freedom and Tenure, 2012-2013.
- Ad hoc reviewer: Campus Research Board, Chancellor's Discovery Fund.
- Reader, Phi Beta Kappa nominations.
- Coordinator, multi-college UIC-UIUC Visiting Speaker Program, sponsored by the UIC Humanities Laboratory 2001-2002.
- Member, Dept. of Communication faculty search committee, 2002.
- Director, Corner for Collaborative Informatics, 2002 – present.
- Member, Chancellor's Committee on LBGT Issues, 2004-2005.
- Member, UIC Health Informatics Task Force, 2002-2006. This is an inter-college committee that reported to Dean Tate.

- Member, Clinical and Translational Science Award (CTSA) Informatics Working Group. UIC received a CTSA planning grant in September 2006, and this multi-college working group was charged with planning and implementing informatics activities to support a CTSA grant application in January 2008 (which received funding through the present).
- Affiliated member, Project Biocultures.
- Department of Psychiatry Review Committee for research involving human subjects, 2008, 2009.

Service for Industry
- Consultant to System Biosciences (SBI), 1616 North Shoreline Blvd., Mountain View, CA.
- Consultant to Acidophil, LLC, 2330 West Joppa Road, Suite 330, Lutherville, MD 21093.

EDUCATIONAL ACTIVITIES
- Instructor, Neuroscience 444, Data Literacy for Neuroscientists, graduate course, 2014 - present. (Created this course and taught solo plus some guest lecturers. Covers experimental design, statistics, laboratory data management and some data mining.) The course notes are the basis for a solo authored textbook "Data Literacy: How to Make your Experiments Robust and Reproducible" now in production at Academic Press (Elsevier), 2017.
- Lecturer in GCLS 502, Molecular Biology, core course for UIC graduate students, lectured on microRNAs (2007-present).

- Instructor, Anatomy/Cell Biology 523, Biology of microRNAs and other Small RNAs, graduate seminar series, 2006, 2009, 2011, 2013, 2015. (Created this course and taught solo.)
- Lecturer in NEUS 501 – Foundations of Neuroscience, graduate course for neuroscience students, November 2013.
- Lecturer in Neuroscience seminar series for psychiatry residents (have lectured on developmental neurobiology) 1999-2013.
- Lecturer in CS 582 - Information Retrieval, graduate course for UIC computer science students, January 2012.
- Lecturer in Biological Sciences 582, graduate course on Experimental Methods in Modern Neuroscience. (have lectured on antibody methods, RNA interference, microRNAs and informatics) 2000-2004; 2008; 2010, 2011.
- Instructor, Honors College core course 134, The Process of Scientific Discovery, 2010 (Created this course and taught solo.)
- Lecturer in Introduction to Biological Psychiatry course for PGY-1 psychiatry residents 2006-2010.
- Lecturer in Graduate course at UIUC, Graduate School of Library and Information Science, "Literature Based Discovery", October 2008.
- Laboratory supervisor in Medical Neuroanatomy course for 1st year medical students 1997-2005

- Organizer and lecturer in 3 day workshop at UIC, "Informatics Tools for Discovery and Collaboration," 9/03, 9/04.
- Lecturer in Anatomy/Cell Biology 520, graduate course on Synaptic Structure and Function (2000, 2001).
- Lecturer in Biological Sciences 286, Biology of Brain (lectured on neurobiology of schizophrenia) (2001, 2002).
- Supervisor of undergraduate students in Biological Sciences 299 and 399 and volunteer research rotations. Logan Grewal, 1998. Mauli Verma, 1999. Rima Patel, 2002 (now a graduate student at UIC School of Public Health). Cristina Floreani, 2003 (now a MD-PhD student at UIC in Anatomy/Cell Biology). Atena Lodhi, 2004.
- Sponsor of high school students:
  - Illinois Math and Science Academy, Student Inquiry and Research Program: Kinga Wilewska, 2004-2005. Kyle Schirmann, 2006-2007. Matthew Liu, 2007-2008.
  - Sidharth Addepalli, summer 2018.
- Mentor of Honors College undergraduate students, 2009-present.
- Mentor of undergraduate students for independent study: Octavio Gomes, 2014.
- Sponsor of postdoctoral fellows:
  Marc Weeber, PhD, 2001-2002, now working in industry (Knewco, Inc.).
- Supervisor of graduate research assistants:

Wei Zhou, 2002-2008. Wei obtained the best results (out of 30 entries nationwide) in the 2006 Genomics TREC competition. First working at Ingenuity Systems, Inc., currently founder and CEO of SeekQuence, Inc.
Wei Zhang, 2002-2006. Now working at Microsoft.
Giovanni Lugli, PhD, 2001-2013, Research Specialist in Health Sciences in my laboratory. With my support and encouragement, he is now enrolled in the Neuroscience Training Program as a PhD candidate at UIC, while continuing to work full-time in my laboratory. His thesis project concerns localization and processing of microRNA precursors within mature forebrain neurons; successfully defended his thesis on 5/19/11.
Yufang Peng, November 4-29, 2016, is a PhD student at Nanjing University School of Information Management, visited my laboratory with support from a Short-Term Graduate Fellowship from Nanjing University.
Mengqi Luo, November 1, 2018 – October 31, 2019, is a PhD student at Wuhan University School of Information Management, is visiting on a fellowship from Wuhan University.
Revathy Venukuttan, January 2019- January 2020, is a Masters student in Bioengineering at UIC. Her sponsor is Bhaskar DasGupta, and I was co-sponsor.

- Member of PhD thesis examination committee:

Wei Zhou, 2008.
James Gocel, 2009.
Sachin Moonat, 2009.
Dina Beeler-Muscat, 2015-present.
Adam Kehoe, 2016 (external member at GS-LIS, UIUC).
Stephanie Muscat, 2017 (external member at Rhode Island School of Design).

- Professional mentoring:
  - Vetle Torvik, PhD, 2001-2008, was Research Assistant Professor in my laboratory. He is developing his own line of research concerned with analyses of collaboration behavior of MEDLINE authors, and was recipient of a Summer Faculty fellowship at the National Center for Supercomputing Applications, working under Noshir Contractor. Vetle is now Assistant Professor at UIUC. Using the Author-ity author name disambiguation dataset developed at UIC, he successfully wrote a NSF grant proposal to merge Author-ity with a disambiguated US Patent database (with Lee Fleming, Harvard Business School, dual PI), beginning in 2010. We are currently both collaborators on a program project sponsored through the National Bureau of Economic Research.
  - Carole L. Palmer, PhD. Dr. Palmer is now Professor at University of Washington Information School. I invited her to undertake the study of information-seeking behavior in the

Arrowsmith field testers, which has developed into a NSF-funded 3 year grant that she directed.

- Ramin Homayouni, PhD. Dr. Homayouni is now Professor at University of Memphis, where he now chairs the Bioinformatics Program. I assisted his informatics efforts during the period when he was a subcontract PI on my Arrowsmith grant.

- Hong Yu, PhD. Dr. Yu is now Professor at University of Massachusetts Medical School. I have been assisting her in writing R01 grants (am listed as a subcontract PI on an upcoming grant of hers submitted in March 2007) and in finding biologists to collaborate with in the development of biology-oriented information retrieval systems.

- Larissa Nonn, PhD. Dr. Nonn is Assistant Professor at UIC who studies the involvement of microRNAs in prostate cancer. I contributed a letter of support for her successful NCI Transition Career Development Award (K22), and am currently a collaborator on her American Cancer Society grant.

- Sandra DeGroote, Professor and Scholarly Communications Librarian at UIC. After she had a research article rejected twice from PloS ONE, I helped her by reanalyzing the data and extending the analysis substantially. The resulting paper was not only published but won the 2016 Ida and George Eliot Prize of the Medical Library Association.

- Byron Wallace, PhD, Assistant Professor in the School of Information at University of Texas, Austin. I invited him to collaborate on our Evidence-Based Medicine grant renewal (2015).
- Siddhartha Jonnalagadda, PhD, Assistant Professor, Northwestern University Medical School, recently moved to Microsoft. I have provided informal mentoring for several years.
- Jodi Schneider, PhD, Assistant Professor, iSchool at University of Illinois at Urbana-Champaign. I invited her to collaborate on our R01 project on evidence-based medicine and am mentoring her own independent research efforts.
- Participant as a Mentor in the American Medical Informatics Association Mentorship program. 2012 mentee: Bishnu Devkota, MD, of St. Louis University.
- Participant as a Mentor in the Winter Brain Conference mentorship program. 2013 mentee: Stephan Lammel, PhD, of Stanford University.
- Participant as a Mentor in the American Medical Informatics Association Mentorship program. 2017 mentee: Kaplana Reddy, MD, Northwell Health, Mineola, NY.
- Participant as a Mentor in the New Leaders program of American Society for Information Science and Technology. 2018 mentee: Nushrat Khan.
- Yakub Sebastian, PhD, Lecturer at Charles Darwin University, co-organized the First

International Workshop on Literature-Based Discovery at PAKKD 2020, and mentoring him for research and funding advice.

- Department of Anatomy & Cell Biology, member of PhD thesis advisory committee for Paul Kim.
- Faculty Medical advisor for William Ruzicka, Anita Seibold.
- Participant in Medical and MD-PhD admissions interviews.
- Member, MD/PhD Program training faculty, Neuroscience PhD program and Biomedical Neuroscience training program, and the Graduate College.
- Fellow, UIC Honors College, 2009-present.

CURRICULUM DESIGN ACTIVITIES
Advisory Committee Member for The Scientific Communications Initiative, 2006-2009. This is a NSF-funded curriculum grant in bioinformatics centered at the Graduate School of Library and Information Science at University of Illinois Urbana-Champaign. PIs are Carole Palmer and P. Bryan Heidorn. The Scientific Communications Initiative is developing a biological informatics masters degree program for Scientific Communication Specialists (SCS). Unlike most existing educational programs in bioinformatics, the SCS program takes a broad view of biology and informatics to train professionals to bridge arenas of information technology development in the biological sciences. Other advisory committee members are chosen nationally from a variety of institutions including the

American Museum of Natural History, the Smithsonian Institution, the Missouri Botanical Garden, the Peabody Museum at Yale, and the Biomedical Informatics Research Network.

INVITED PRESENTATIONS
Invited Presentations at International Conferences since 1996:

- Lecturer, Green College Thematic Lecture Series on Creativity, University of British Columbia, Vancouver, Canada, January 2002. This is a University-wide event inviting distinguished visitors from around the world, and the lectures are collected and published in book form by University of Toronto Press.

- Organizer, workshop on Informatics, Intl. Congress for Schizophrenia Research, Colorado Springs, March 2003.

- Organizer, workshop on "Informatics for Neurochemists," Intl. Soc. Neurochemistry meeting, Hong Kong, August 2003. (Meeting cancelled because of SARS epidemic.)

- Organizer, technology panel on MicroRNAs and RNA Interference in the Nervous System, Asian-Pacific Society for Neurochemistry Biennial Meeting, Hong Kong, February 2004.

- Speaker, panel on "Mining the Literature to Promote Biomedical Discoveries" at Medinfo [International Medical Informatics Association triennial meeting], San Francisco, September 2004.

- Plenary speaker and session chair, 8th International Conference on Discovery Science, Singapore, October 2005.
- Discussant, First Monday FM10 Openness Conference, Chicago, May 2006.
- Speaker, Workshop on Scholarly Databases & Data Integration, Bloomington, IN, August 2006.
- Discussant, Pacific Symposium on Biocomputing, Maui, HI, January 2007.
- Speaker, T-FaNT 07 (Tokyo Forum on Advanced NLP and Text Mining), Tokyo, Japan, March 2007.
- Co-organizer, workshop on Fragile X protein/microRNA pathways in neurons, International Society for Neurochemistry biennial meeting, Cancun, August 2007 (meeting canceled due to Hurricane Dean).
- Chair and speaker, symposium on Non-coding RNAs and Synaptic Plasticity, International Society for Neurochemistry biennial meeting, Athens, Greece, August 2011.
- Speaker, International Congress of Human Genetics, Oct. 11 - 15, 2011, Montreal, session on "Functional genomics of long non-coding RNA in mammalian systems."
- Organizer and tutorial speaker, 5th ACM Conference on Bioinformatics, Computational Biology, and Health Informatics, Newport Beach, CA, USA, September 20-23, 2014.

- Invited speaker, Symposium on Automation and Systematic Reviews, Bristol, UK, November 11-12, 2015.
- Invited speaker, Data-Driven Discovery: Data Science meets Information Science, Chinese Academy of Sciences, Beijing, China, June 19-22, 2016.
- Invited speaker, 3rd International Collaboration for the Automation of Systematic Reviews (ICASR) workshop, London, England, October 17-18, 2017; 5th Annual Workshop, Bergen, Norway, 2019.
- Keynote speaker, 8th International Workshop on Mining Scientific Publications (WOSP 2020), Wuhan, China, 2020.

Invited Presentations at National Conferences since 1996:
- Speaker, Society for Neuroscience Satellite Meeting on the Human Brain Project, November 2002.
- Organizer, panel session on Literature-Based Discovery, Am. Soc. For Information Science and Technology, Washington, DC, October 2003.
- Speaker, Short Course on Bioinformatics, Society for Neuroscience meeting, New Orleans, LA, November 2003.
- Speaker, symposium on RNA interference at the Am. Soc. Neurochemistry annual meeting, NYC, August 2004.
- Speaker, Cambridge Healthtech Institute conference on RNA Interference, San Francisco, June 2005.

- Speaker, panel on ""Enabling Biomedical Research with Literature Access and Mining: Progress and Challenges," American Medical Informatics Association annual meeting, Washington, DC, October 2005.
- Speaker, panel on "Literature-based Discovery," American Medical Informatics Association annual Spring Congress, Phoenix, AZ, May 2006.
- Panelist, NIH Knowledge Environments for Biomedical Research (KEBR) Conference, Bethesda, Maryland, December 2006.
- Speaker, meeting on Unique Identifiers for Authors/Contributors sponsored by CrossRef, Washington, DC, February 2007.
- Speaker, Cambridge Healthtech Institute conference on microRNA in Human Disease & Development, Boston, MA, March 2007.
- Speaker, PubMed Plus conference, sponsored by the Society for Neuroscience, St. Louis, MO, June 2007.
- Participant, NSF Biomedical Informatics workshop, Portland, OR, December 2007.
- Speaker, Symposium on Computational Approaches to Creativity in Science, Stanford, CA, March 2008.
- Participant, IARPA M^2 Conference on Technical Discovery, Extraction and Organization, Northbrook, IL, October 2008.
- Speaker, Cambridge Healthtech Institute conference on microRNA in Human Disease & Development, Boston, MA, March 2009.

- Speaker, panel: Beyond (simple) Reading: Strategies, Discoveries, and Collaborations, Am. Soc. For Information Science and Technology, Vancouver, BC, November 2009.
- Participant, "Integrating, Representing, and Reasoning over Human Knowledge: A Computational Grand Challenge for the 21st Century," August 7-14, 2010, at the Snowbird Ski and Summer Resort Conference Center, hosted by the Institute for Computing in Science (ICiS).
- Organizer of panel and discussant, "Tools for Identifying Reliable Evidence and Implementing it in Everyday Clinical Care," March 2013, at the AMIA Joint Summits on Translational Science (Clinical Research Informatics), San Francisco, CA.
- Invited participant, CHDI Foundation workshop, "Sources and Potential Uses of Exosomes in Huntington's Disease Therapeutics," New York City, May 2013.
- Invited symposium speaker, Medical Library Association, May 20, 2014.
- Organizer of panel, "ClinicalTrials.gov: Adding Value through Informatics," AMIA Annual Symposium, November 2015, San Francisco, CA.
- Invited speaker, 2nd Annual Next Generation Sequencing and Single Cell Analysis USA Congress, 3-4 October 2016, Boston, MA.

Invited Presentations within UIC since 1996:
- Dept. of Anatomy & Cell Biology, 1996.

- College of Medicine, MD-PhD Training Program, March 2005.
- Honors 201 Seminar, "Networks in Life Sciences," March 2006.
- Autism Study Group, February 2009.
- Panel on Open Access journals, Daley Library, October 2009.
- Frontiers of GI Research Conference, February 2012.
- Biomedical and Health Informatics Colloquium, part of Chicago Informatics Week, October 2012.
- Center for Pharmaceutical Biotechnology seminar series, December 2012.
- Biomedical and Health Informatics Colloquium, September 2015.
- Data Blitz, Research Extravaganza, September 2018.
- Lightning talks in Data Science, August 7, 2020.

Invited Presentations at other Universities since 1996:
- Northwestern Univ. Medical School, 1996.
- Univ. Florida at Gainesville Dept. of Pharmacology, 1996.
- Chicago Institute for Neurosurgery and Neuroresearch, 1996.
- Second Intl. Oxidative Stress and Brain Damage Symposium, 1997.
- UIUC, Graduate Library and Information Sciences School, 2001.
- UIUC, Beckman Institute, 2002.

- Stanford Univ., Division of Child and Adolescent Psychiatry, November 2002.
- Tennessee Bioinformatics Consortium, March 2004.
- Michigan State Univ., Dept. of Pharmacology and Toxicology, September 2004.
- RIKEN Biological Resource Center, Tsukuba, Japan, October 2005.
- University of Wisconsin-Milwaukee, Medical Informatics program, February 2007.
- Chicago Biomedical Consortium, RNA Symposium, June 2007.
- Chicagoland RNA Club, Feburary 2008.
- Merck Serono (Research Knowledge Management), Geneva, Switzerland and Darmstadt, Germany, June 2008.
- Harvard Business School, Science-Based Business Initiative Seminar, February 2009.
- Jefferson Medical College, The RNA Matters Lecture Series, June 14, 2011.
- Penn State University, distinguished lecture on discovery informatics, April 28, 2014.
- Indiana University, Department of Information and Library Science, ILS Spring Colloquium, May 1, 2015.
- Loyola University Medical School, Psychiatry Grand Rounds, January 14, 2016.
- Lutheran General Hospital, Psychiatry Grand Rounds, May 25, 2016.

- Wuhan University, School of Information Management, June 15, 2016.
- Wuhan University, School of Information Management, visiting and giving a series of lectures April 7-28, 2017.
- Yonsei University, Seoul, South Korea, School of Information Science, October 11, 2017.

GRANTS
(active grants are indicated in **bold**)

- NIH NRSA individual postdoctoral training award, National Eye Institute, 1984-1985. Smalheiser, N. R., PI.
- Block Fund grant (University of Chicago), 1986. Smalheiser, N. R., PI.
- Brain Research Foundation grants, 1984-1987, 1993. Smalheiser, N. R., PI.
- Dysautonomia Foundation grants, 1986-1988. Smalheiser, N. R., PI.
- March of Dimes Basil O'Connor Starter Scholar award, 1987-1989. Smalheiser, N. R., PI.
- March of Dimes, "Laminin as a molecular and genetic probe of neurites," 1990-1992. Smalheiser, N. R., PI.
- NIH FIRST award, "Molecular and cellular basis of cranin's action on neural cells," 1988-1992. Smalheiser, N. R., PI.

- Scottish Rite Schizophrenia Research Program, "Heat shock protein 60 serum antibodies in schizophrenia," 1993-1994. Smalheiser, N. R., PI.
- NIH Program Project, "Biological basis of mental retardation," National Institute for Child Health and Human Development, 1992-1995. Schwartz, N. B., PI. (I was Project P.I. of Project #2).
- Office of Naval Research, "ARROWSMITH Analysis of Biomedical Innovation and Discovery," 1999-2000 ($50,000 direct costs). We were specifically invited to write this application by the ONR. Smalheiser, N. R., PI.
- NIH R03, "Circulating Reelin and Psychosis Vulnerability," National Institute of Mental Health; 9/00-8/02. ($50,000 direct costs per year for 2 years). Smalheiser, N. R., PI.
- National Alliance for Autism Research, "Circulating Reelin and Autism Spectrum Disorder," 7/01-6/03 ($45,000 direct costs per year for 2 years). Smalheiser, N. R., PI.
- NIH R01, "Arrowsmith Data Mining Techniques in Neuro-Informatics," 6/01-5/07. Human Brain Project grant, co-funded by NLM and NIMH. Funded on the first submission. (This is a large grant representing a multi-institutional consortium of six sites, of which UIC is the home site. The overall budget is $500,000 direct costs per year for five years.) Smalheiser, N. R., PI.
- NIH R21, "RNAi-Mediated Gene Suppression in the Adult Mammalian CNS," National Institute of Drug Abuse; 9/30/02-9/30/05 ($100,000 direct costs per

year for 2 years, currently on no-cost extension). This is a CEBRA grant funded by NIDA for "cutting-edge" innovative high-risk, high-payoff investigations. Funded on the first submission. Smalheiser, N. R., PI.

- NIH R21, "Author Name Disambiguation in Medline," National Library of Medicine; 1/15/05 – 6/30/08. $125,000 direct costs per year. Funded on the first submission. This is an effort to disambiguate authors (many different people may have the same last name, first initial). We will assign all articles in Medline in clusters according to the individuals who wrote them. Smalheiser, N. R., PI.

- NIH R01, "Function of FMRP in the mouse olfactory system," National Institute of Deafness and Other Communications Disorders; 07/01/03 – 06/30/08 Larson J., PI (N. Smalheiser, co-I, 10% effort). $175,000 direct costs per year for five years. This is a grant to study the role of the fragile X mental retardation protein in olfactory perception and memory.

- High Q Foundation, "Literature-Based Discovery Techniques to Identify Novel Huntington Disease Modifiers, Treatments or Targets", 8/15/07 – 2/14/08, Smalheiser, N. R., PI., $24,000 direct costs.

- NIH R21, "Validating microRNA Analysis in Human Postmortem Brain" (Y. Dwivedi, N. Smalheiser, dual PIs). National Institute of Mental Health, 7/1/07 – 6/30/09, $125,000 direct costs per year for 2 years requested. Funded on the first submission.

- Stanley Medical Research Institute proposal, "Prefrontal Cortex microRNAs in the Stanley Neuropathology Consortium," Smalheiser, N. R., PI, $75,000 per year for 2 years. 8/1/08-7/31/11.
- Alzheimer's Association, IIRG-11-202853, "Plasma microRNAs as biomarkers for Alzheimer disease," Smalheiser, N. R., PI. 11/1/11 – 4/30/15. total $200,000 direct costs.
- Dept. of the Army – USAMRAA, "Cellular Basis for Learning Impairment in Fragile X Syndrome," Larson, J. R., PI. 04/01/2012 - 03/31/2015. $750,000 direct costs per year for 3 years. My role is co-Investigator.
- University of Illinois at Chicago CCTS-0512-03, "Plasma Small RNAs as Biomarkers for Pediatric Bipolar Disorder", Dwivedi, Y., PI. 5/1/12 – 4/30/14. $30,000 direct costs per year for two years. My role is co-PI.
- **NIH R01, LM010817-01, "Text Mining Pipeline to Accelerate Systematic Reviews in Evidence-Based Medicine," Smalheiser, N. R. and Cohen, A.M., dual PIs. This is a multi-institutional consortium encompassing 4 sites, of which UIC is home site. About $442,000 direct costs per year for 4 years. 9/30/2010 – 9/29/15. Funded on the first submission. Renewal application submitted 11/5/15, received a priority score in the top 3% and was funded. New period is 7/05/2016 – 6/30/2020. About $390,000 direct costs per year for 4 years.**

- American Cancer Society – Research Scholar Award, "Vitamin D reverses global repression of microRNAs in prostate cancer", Nonn, L., PI. 1/1/2013-12/31/2016. My role is co-Investigator.
- **NIH NIA P01 AG039347, "Innovation in an Aging Society". Bruce Weinberg, PI. 9/30/2013-6/30/2018. UIC direct costs for year 1 = $86,449. My role is co-Investigator. A one-year supplement grant has also been given to supplement this work, 9/30/17-8/31/18 and another 9/30/18 – 8/31/19.**
- New Venture Fund / Robert Wood Johnson Foundation, "BiAffect - the Mood Challenge for ResearchKit", Alex Leow and Peter Nelson, PIs. 10/2016-8/2017. My role is co-Investigator. This won the Grand Prize of the Mood Challenge.
- Pending: NIH NLM   1 T15 9264277, Chicago Initiative for Biomedical Informatics and Data Science Training (CIBIDS)

Role: Primary Mentor [no faculty recovery salary; multi PI: JB Starren (NU), AL Valenta (UIC), S Volchenboum (UC)]

Total Project Period   07/01/2017 – 06/30/2022

Total Costs $7,702,067

The purpose of the grant is to advance the training of future Biomedical Informatics and Data Science (BIDS) Researchers through the Chicago Initiative for Biomedical Informatics and Data Science Training (CIBIDS), a joint effort of three major institutions in the Chicago area—Northwestern University (NU),

University of Illinois at Chicago (UIC), and University of Chicago (UC).

PATENTS, INVENTIONS AND COMMERCIALIZATION

Developer of two monoclonal antibodies against cranin (dystroglycan) that were licensed commercially by Chemicon.

Co-developer, with Don R. Swanson (Univ. of Chicago), of ARROWSMITH, a computer-assisted strategy for information retrieval.

Co-developer, with Vetle Torvik, of Author-ity, which utilizes a new monotone Boolean method of data mining. The Author-ity database is a resource that disambiguates author names for papers in MEDLINE. Licensed to NIH (NCBI) in 2009. Licensed to LnxResearch in 2009. Other licenses pending.

Co-developer, with Vetle Torvik, of ADAM, a database of abbreviations in Medline that includes both acronyms and non-acronyms.

Developer of WETLAB, an open source electronic notebook programmed in JAVA.

Co-developer, with Vetle Torvik, of Anne O'Tate, which facilitates summarization, drill-down and browsing of PubMed search results.

Co-developer, with Vetle Torvik, of a novel quantitative model to measure the type and amount of implicit information linking two sets of articles. Licensed to Merck Serono in 2008.

Co-developer, with Yogesh Dwivedi, of a use patent application for enoxacin and related agents as anti-depressants and for treatment of PTSD. Filed December 2013.

Press Coverage:
Profiled in *The Scientist* 12: 12-13, 1998.
Profiled in *Science* magazine 310: 1401, 2005.
Mentioned in an editorial in *Nature* magazine 440: 1090, 2006.
Genetic Engineering & Biotechnology News (http://www.genengnews.com/) rated the Arrowsmith Project website "Excellent" in their Best of the Web: Reference" list, December 2007.
Profiled/interviewed in *Biomedical Computation Review* 4: 16-27, 2008.
Mentioned in a news feature in *Nature* magazine 463: 416-418, 2010.
Our abstract on endogenous siRNAs was chosen by Society for Neuroscience as a "Hot Topic" in their 2010 Annual Meeting.
Our study of miRNA expression in depressed suicide patients was profiled by *The Daily*, July, 2012.
Our 2012 study of synaptic primary miRNA transcripts was recommended by Faculty of 1000.
Our 2014 study of enoxacin and learned helplessness was highlighted in a Frontiers in Psychiatry

commentary:
http://journal.frontiersin.org/article/10.3389/fpsyt.2015.0
0044/full.
Our 2015 study of miRNA expression in exosomal
fractions of plasma in Alzheimer's patients vs. controls
was profiled by The Scientist. http://www.the-
scientist.com/?articles.view/articleNo/45583/title/Writte
n-in-Blood/
In addition, I have been interviewed as an expert source
to comment on my own or others' work for various
online news stories (e.g. *Nature*, Medicine Online, The
Discovery Channel, *The Scientist*, *Biomedical
Computation Review*, MyScienceWork, *Nature
Medicine*, etc.)

PUBLICATIONS (name is in bold if senior author)
H-Index (based on Google Scholar) = 52.
A note on journals:
The publications span numerous specialties both within
biomedical research and information sciences, and
recording impact factor is misleading because different
fields vary significantly in the impact factor of their
leading journals. However, Journal of Biological
Chemistry is the most important journal in the field of
biochemistry; PNAS is one of the top 5 general-interest
scientific journals; Artificial Intelligence is the leading
journal in its field; Archives of General Psychiatry is the
#2 journal in psychiatry; Trends in Neurosciences has
the highest impact factor in neuroscience; Journal of the
American Society for Information Science and
Technology is the most prestigious journal in
information science; JAMIA has the highest impact

factor in medical informatics; The New England Journal of Medicine is the leading general-interest journal in medicine; PLOS Biology is the leading general-interest open access journal in biology; and Trends in Genetics is one of the top journals in genetics. Annual Review of Information Science and Technology is the most prestigious review journal in its field. Finally, note that the lab generally presents 2-4 abstracts at meetings each year; however, they are not listed in this curriculum vitae because they are not mature publications.

A note on author order:
We follow the convention of many biomedical laboratories, in which the person who acquires the primary data in a study and prepares the figures and tables is listed as first author. Often, but not always, this person is also the one who wrote the first draft of the paper. Other authors are listed in order of their relative contributions, except the PI who is generally listed last. This does not imply that the PI has a relatively minor role or is listed as a courtesy.

A note on open access:
Since the launching of PubMed Central, BioMed Central and Public Library of Science, my policy has been to publish articles in open access journals and/or post preprints whenever possible.

PEER REVIEWED PUBLICATIONS

1. Smalheiser, N. R. and Crain, S. M. (1978) Formation of functional retinotectal connections in co-cultures of fetal mouse explants. Brain Res. 148: 484-492.

2. Smalheiser, N. R., Crain, S. M., and Bornstein, M. B. (1981) Development of ganglion cells and their axons in organized cultures of fetal mouse retinal explants. Brain Res. 204: 159-178.

3. Smalheiser, N. R., Peterson, E. R., and Crain, S. M. (1981) Neurites from mouse retina and dorsal root ganglion explants show specific behavior within co-cultured tectum or spinal cord. Brain Res. 208: 499-505.

4. Smalheiser, N. R., Peterson, E. R., and Crain, S. M. (1981) Specific neurite pathways and arborizations formed by fetal mouse dorsal root ganglion cells within organized spinal cord explants in culture: a peroxidase labeling study. Dev. Brain Res. 2: 383-396.

5. Smalheiser, N. R. (1982) Positional specificity tests in co-cultures of retinal and tectal explants. Brain Res. 213: 493-499.

6. Smalheiser, N. R., Crain, S. M., and Reid, L. M. (1984) Laminin as a substrate for retinal axons in vitro. Dev. Brain Res. 12: 136-140.

7. Smalheiser, N. R. and Crain, S. M. (1984) Radiosensitivity and differentiation of retinal ganglion cells within fetal mouse explants in vitro. Dev. Brain Res. 13: 159-163.

8. **Smalheiser**, N. R. and Crain, S. M. (1984) The possible role of "sibling neurite bias" in the coordination of neurite elongation, branching, and survival. J. Neurobiol. 15: 517-529.

9. **Smalheiser**, N. R. and Schwartz, N. B. (1987) Cranin: a laminin binding protein of cell membranes. Proc. Natl. Acad. Sci. USA 84: 6457-6461.

10. **Smalheiser**, N. R. and Schwartz, N. B. (1987) Kinetic analysis of 'rapid onset' neurite formation in NG108-15 cells reveals a dual role for substratum-bound laminin. Dev. Brain Res. 34: 111-121.

11. Schwartz, N. B. and Smalheiser, N. R. (1989) Biosynthesis of glycosaminoglycans and proteoglycans. In: Neurobiology of Glycoconjugates, ed. R.U. and R.K. Margolis, Plenum Press, NY, pp. 151-186.

12. **Smalheiser**, N. R. (1989) Morphologic plasticity of rapid-onset neurites in NG108-15 cells stimulated by substratum-bound laminin. Dev. Brain Res. 45: 39-47.

13. **Smalheiser**, N. R. (1989) Analysis of slow-onset neurite formation in NG108-15 cells: implications for a unified model of neurite elongation. Dev. Brain Res. 45: 49-57.

14. **Smalheiser**, N. R. (1989) Altered cell shapes in mouse 3T3 fibroblasts treated with 5'-deoxy, 5'-methyl

thioadenosine: relation to morphogenesis of neural cells. Dev. Brain Res. 45: 59-67.

15. **Smalheiser**, N. R. (1990) Neuronal growth cones: an extended view. Neuroscience 38: 1-11.

16. **Smalheiser**, N. R. (1990) Cell attachment and neurite stability in NG108-15 cells: effects of 5'-deoxy, 5'-methyl thioadenosine (MTA) compared with laminin, kinase inhibitor H-7, and Mn^{2+} ions. Dev. Brain Res. 51: 153-160.

17. **Smalheiser**, N. R. (1990) Cell attachment and neurite stability in NG108-15 cells: What is the role of microtubules? Dev. Brain Res. 58: 271-282.

18. **Smalheiser**, N. R. (1991) Role of laminin in stimulating rapid-onset neurites in NG108-15 cells: relative contribution of attachment and motility responses. Dev. Brain Res. 62: 81-89.

19. Pomeranz, H. D., Sherman, D. L., Smalheiser, N. R. and Gershon, M. D. (1991) Expression of the immunoreactivity of a neurally related cell surface laminin binding protein by neural crest-derived cells migrating to and within the gut: relationship to the formation of enteric ganglia. J. Comp. Neurol. 313: 625-642.

20. **Smalheiser**, N. R. and Collins, B. J. (1992) Characterization of a novel set of membrane antigens

associated with axonal growth. I: Biochemical and functional studies. Dev. Brain Res. 69: 215-223.

21. **Smalheiser**, N. R. and Collins, B. J. (1992) Characterization of a novel set of membrane antigens associated with axonal growth. II: Expression in the chick central nervous system. Dev. Brain Res. 69: 225-231.

22. **Smalheiser**, N. R., Collins, B. J., and Sharma, S. C. (1992) Characterization of a novel set of membrane antigens associated with axonal growth. III: Expression in the regenerating goldfish optic nerve and tectum. Dev. Brain Res. 69: 277-282.

23. **Smalheiser**, N. R. and Rossulek, M. (1992) Morphometric and time lapse analyses of rapid-onset neurites stimulated by cycloheximide in NG108-15 cells. Int. J. Dev. Neurosci. 10: 467-472.

24. Landis, C. A., Collins, B. J., Cribbs, L. L., Sukhatme, V., Bergmann, B., Rechtschaffen, A., and **Smalheiser**, N. R. (1993) Expression of EGR-1 in the brain of sleep-deprived rats. Molec. Brain Res. 17: 300-306.

25. **Smalheiser**, N. R. (1993) Monensin-sensitive cellular events modulate neurite extension on laminin: an example of higher order regulation of cell motility. Cell Motil. Cytoskel. 24: 256-263.

26. **Smalheiser**, N. R. (1993) Acute neurite retraction elicited by diverse agents is prevented by genistein, a tyrosine kinase inhibitor. J. Neurochem. 61: 340-343.

27. **Smalheiser**, N. R. (1993) Cranin interacts specifically with the sulfatide-binding domain of laminin. J. Neurosci. Res. 36: 528-538.

28. **Smalheiser**, N. R. and Swanson, D. R. (1994) Assessing a gap in the biomedical literature: magnesium deficiency and neurologic disease. Neurosci. Res. Commun. 15: 1-9.

29. **Smalheiser**, N. R. and Ali, J. Y. (1994) Acute neurite retraction triggered by lysophosphatidic acid: timing of the inhibitory effects of genistein. Brain Res. 660: 309-318.

30. **Smalheiser**, N. R. (1994) Three good things about "bad" science. Perspect. Biol. Med. 38: 58-60.

31. **Smalheiser**, N. R., Dissanayake, S. and Kapil, A. (1995) Regulation of neurite outgrowth and retraction by phospholipase A_2-derived arachidonic acid and its metabolites. Brain Res. 721: 39-48, 1996.

32. **Smalheiser**, N. R. and Kim, E. (1995) Purification of cranin, a laminin binding protein. Identity to dystroglycan and reassessment of its carbohydrate moieties. J. Biol. Chem. 270: 15425-15433.

33. **Smalheiser**, N. R. (1996) Proteins in unexpected locations. Molec. Biol. Cell 7: 1003-1014.

34. Belkin, A. M. and **Smalheiser**, N. R. (1996) Localization of cranin (dystroglycan) at sites of cell-matrix and cell-cell contact: recruitment to focal adhesions is dependent upon extracellular ligands. Cell Adhes. Commun. 4: 281-296.

35. **Smalheiser**, N. R. (1996) The importance of parametric approaches in the analysis of cell behavior. Perspect. Biol. Med. 40: 60-65.

36. **Smalheiser**, N. R. and Swanson, D. R. (1996) Indomethacin and Alzheimer's disease. Neurology 46: 583.

37. **Smalheiser**, N. R. and Swanson, D. R. (1996) Linking estrogen to Alzheimer's disease: an informatics approach. Neurology 47: 809-810.

38. Swanson, D. R. and Smalheiser, N. R. (1997) An interactive system for finding complementary literatures: a stimulus to scientific discovery. Artif. Intell. 91: 183-203.

39. Peng, H. B., Ali, A. A., Daggett, D. F., Rauvala, H., Hassell, J. R., and **Smalheiser**, N. R. (1998) The relationship between perlecan and dystroglycan and its implication in the formation of the neuromuscular junction. Cell Adhes. Commun. 5: 475-489.

40. **Smalheiser**, N. R. and Swanson, D. R. (1998) Calcium-independent phospholipase A_2 and schizophrenia. Arch. Gen. Psychiat. 55: 752-753.

41. **Smalheiser**, N. R. and Swanson, D. R. (1998) Using ARROWSMITH: a computer-assisted approach to formulating and assessing scientific hypotheses. Computer Meth. Prog. Biomed. 57: 149-153.

42. **Swanson D**, Smalheiser N. Link analysis of MEDLINE titles as an aid to scientific discovery. Proceedings of the AAAI Fall Symposium on Artificial Intelligence and Link Analysis 1998 (pp. 94-97).

43. **Smalheiser**, N. R., Haslam, S. M., Sutton-Smith, M., Morris, H. R., and Dell, A. (1998) Structural analysis of sequences O-linked to mannose reveals a novel Lewis X structure in cranin (dystroglycan) purified from sheep brain. J. Biol. Chem. 273: 23698-23703.

44. Impagnatiello, F., Guidotti, A., Pesold, C., Dwivedi, Y., Caruncho, H., Pisu, M.G., Uzunov, D.P., Smalheiser, N.R., Davis, J.M., Pandey, G.N., Pappas, G.D., Tueting, P., Sharma, R.P. and Costa, E. (1998) A decrease in reelin expression as a putative vulnerability factor in schizophrenia. Proc. Natl. Acad. Sci. USA 95: 15718-15723.

45. **Smalheiser**, N. R. (1998) Conserved amphipathic helices near the N-terminus and C-terminus of the alpha subunit of cranin (dystroglycan). Cell Adhes. Commun. 6: 401-404.

46. Swanson, D. R. and Smalheiser, N. R. (1999) Implicit text linkages between Medline records: using Arrowsmith as an aid to scientific discovery. Library Trends 48: 48-59.

47. **Smalheiser**, N. R., Costa, E., Guidotti, A., Impagnatiello, F., Auta, J., Lacor, P., Kriho, V. and Pappas, G. (2000) Expression of reelin in adult mammalian blood, liver, pituitary pars intermedia and adrenal chromaffin cells. Proc. Natl. Acad. Sci. USA 97: 1281-1286.

48. **Smalheiser**, N. R. (2000) Walter Pitts. Perspect. Biol. Med. 43: 217-226.

49. **Smalheiser**, N. R. and Collins, B. J. (2000) Coordinate enrichment of cranin (dystroglycan) subunits in synaptic membranes of sheep brain. Brain Res. 887: 469-471.

50. Manev, H., Uz, T., Smalheiser, N. R. and Manev, R. (2001) Antidepressants alter cell proliferation in the adult brain in vivo and in neural cultures in vitro. Eur. J. Pharmacol. 411: 67-70.

51. **Smalheiser**, N. R., Manev, H. and Costa, E. (2001) RNAi and Memory: Was McConnell on the right track after all? Trends in Neurosci. 24: 216-218.

52. Smalheiser, N. R. (2001) Predicting emerging technologies with the aid of text-based data mining: the micro approach. Technovation 21: 689-693.

53. Swanson, D. R., Smalheiser, N. R. and Bookstein, A. (2001) Information discovery from complementary literatures: categorizing viruses as potential weapons. J. Am. Soc. Information Sci. Technol.52: 797-812.

54. Kim, H.M., Qu, T., Kriho, V., Lacor, P., Smalheiser, N., Pappas, G. D., Guidotti, A., Costa, E. and Sugaya, K. (2002) Reelin function in neural stem cell biology. Proc. Natl. Acad. Sci. USA 99: 4020-4025.

55. Das, A., Smalheiser, N. R., Markaryan, A. and Kaplan, A. (2002) Evidence for binding of the ectodomain of amyloid precursor protein 695 and activated high molecular weight kininogen. Biochimica et Biophysica Acta (General Subjects) 1571: 225-238.

56. Smalheiser, N. R. (2002) Informatics and hypothesis-driven research. EMBO Reports 3: 702.

57. Smalheiser, N. R. (2003) Linking investigators: A centralised linking facility for data sharing and coordination of samples in banks. EMBO Reports 4: 108–110.

58. Dong, E., Caruncho, H., Liu, W.-S., Smalheiser, N. R., Grayson, D. R., Costa, E. and Guidotti, A. (2003) A reelin-integrin receptor interaction regulates Arc mRNA

translation in synaptoneurosomes. Proc. Natl. Acad. Sci. USA 100: 5479-5484.

59. Smalheiser, N. R. (2003) EST analyses predict the existence of a population of chimeric microRNA precursor – mRNA transcripts expressed in normal mouse and human tissue. Genome Biol. 4: 403. http://genomebiology.com/2003/4/7/403

60. Lugli, G., Krueger, J. M., Davis, J.M. Persico, A. M., Keller, F. and **Smalheiser**, N. R. (2003) Methodological factors influencing measurement and processing of plasma reelin in humans. BMC Biochemistry 4: 9. http://www.biomedcentral.com/1471-2091/4/9

61. Gardner D, Toga AW, Ascoli GA, Beatty JT, Brinkley JF, Dale AM, Fox PT, Gardner EP, George JS, Goddard N, Harris KM, Herskovits EH, Hines ML, Jacobs GA, Jacobs RE, Jones EG, Kennedy DN, Kimberg DY, Mazziotta JC, Miller PL, Mori S, Mountain DC, Reiss AL, Rosen GD, Rottenberg DA, Shepherd GM, Smalheiser NR, Smith KP, Strachan T, Van Essen DC, Williams RW, Wong ST. (2003) Towards effective and rewarding data sharing. Neuroinformatics. 1: 289-295.

62. Smalheiser, N. R. (2003) Bath toys: a source of gastrointestinal infection. New Engl J Med. 350: 521.

63. Smalheiser, N. R. and Torvik, V. I. (2004) A population-based statistical approach identifies parameters characteristic of human microRNA-mRNA interactions. BMC Bioinformatics 5:139.

64. Torvik, V. I., Weeber, M., Swanson, D. R. and **Smalheiser**, N. R. (2005) A probabilistic similiarity metric for Medline records: a model for author name disambiguation. J. Am. Soc. Information Sci. Technol. 56: 140-158.

65. **Smalheiser**, N. R. and Torvik, V. I. (2005) Mammalian microRNAs derived from genomic repeats. Trends in Genetics 21: 322-326.

66. Lugli, G., Larson, J., Martone, M.E., Jones Y. and **Smalheiser**, N. R. (2005) Dicer and eIF2c are enriched at postsynaptic densities in adult mouse brain and are modified by neuronal activity in a calpain-dependent manner. J. Neurochem. 94: 896-905.

67. **Smalheiser**, N. R., Perkins, G. A. and Jones, S. (2005) Guidelines for negotiating scientific collaborations. Endorsed by the Am. Medical Informatics Assn. Working Group on Ethical, Legal and Social Issues. PLOS Biology 3: e217.

68. Zhang, W., Yu, C., Smalheiser, N. R. and Torvik, V. I. (2005) Segmentation of Publication Records of Authors from the Web. (poster paper) In the Proceedings of the 22nd IEEE International Conference on Data Engineering (ICDE'06). Atlanta, GA, April 2006. (this conference was peer-reviewed and had overall 31% acceptance rate)

69. **Smalheiser, N. R.** and Torvik, V. I. (2006) Alu elements within human mRNAs are probable microRNA targets. Trends in Genetics 22(10), 532-536.

70. Zhou, W., **Smalheiser, N. R.** and Yu, C. (2006) A tutorial on information retrieval: basic terms and concepts. J. Biomed. Discovery Collaboration 1: 2.

71. **Smalheiser, N. R.,** Torvik, V. I., Bischoff-Grethe, A., Burhans, L. B., Michael Gabriel, M., Homayouni, R., Kashef, A., Martone, M. E., Perkins, G. A., Price, D. L., Talk, A. C. and West, R. (2006) Collaborative development of the Arrowsmith two node search interface designed for laboratory investigators. J. Biomed. Discovery Collaboration 1: 8.

72. Swanson, D. R., Smalheiser, N. R. and Torvik, V. I. (2006) Ranking indirect connections in literature-based discovery: The role of Medical Subject Headings (MeSH). J. Am. Soc. Information Sci. Technol. 57: 1427-1439.

73. Zhou, W., Torvik, V. I. and **Smalheiser, N. R.** (2006) ADAM: Another database of abbreviations in MEDLINE. Bioinformatics 22: 2813-2818.

74. Zhou, W., Yu, C., Smalheiser, N., Torvik, V. and Hong, J. (2007) Knowledge-intensive Conceptual Retrieval and Passage Extraction of Biomedical Literature. Proc. 30th Ann. Intl. ACM SIGIR Conf. on Research & Development on Information

Retrieval(SIGIR'07), pp. 655-662, 2007, Amsterdam, Netherlands (this conference was peer-reviewed and had overall 18% acceptance rate).

75. Torvik, V. I. and **Smalheiser, N. R.** (2007) A quantitative model for linking two disparate literatures in MEDLINE. Bioinformatics 23(13): 1658-1665.

76. **Smalheiser, N. R.** and Torvik, V. I. (2008) Author name disambiguation. Annual Review of Information Science and Technology 43: 287-313.

77. **Smalheiser, N. R.** (2007) Exosomal transfer of proteins and RNAs at synapses in the nervous system. Biology Direct 2:35.

78. **Smalheiser, N. R.,** Zhou, W. and Torvik, V. I. (2008) Anne O'Tate: A tool to support user-driven summarization, drill-down and browsing of PubMed search results. J. Biomed. Discovery Collab. 3:2.

79. **Smalheiser, N. R** (2008) Regulation of microRNA processing and function by cellular signaling and subcellular localization. Biochim. Biophys. Acta Gene Regulatory Mechanisms 1779:678-681.

80. Lugli, G., Torvik, V.I., Larson, J.R. and **Smalheiser, N. R.** (2008) Expression of microRNAs and their precursors in synaptic fractions of adult mouse forebrain. J. Neurochem 106: 650-661.

81. **Smalheiser, N. R.** (2008) Synaptic enrichment of microRNAs is related to structural features of their precursors. Biology Direct 3: 44.

82. **Smalheiser, N.R.**, Lugli, G., Torvik, V.I., Mise, N., Ikeda, R. and Abe, K. (2008) Natural antisense transcripts are co-expressed with sense mRNAs in synaptoneurosomes of adult mouse forebrain. Neurosci. Res. 62: 236-239.

83. **Smalheiser, N. R.,** Torvik, V.I. and Zhou, W. (2009) Arrowsmith two-node search interface: a tutorial on finding meaningful links between two disparate sets of articles in MEDLINE. Comput. Meth. Programs Biomed. 94: 190-197.

84. Torvik, V. I. and Smalheiser, N. R. (2009) Author name disambiguation in MEDLINE. ACM Transactions on Knowledge Discovery from Data 3(3):11.

85. **Smalheiser, N. R**. and Lugli, G. (2009) microRNA regulation of synaptic plasticity. NeuroMolecular Medicine 11: 133-140.

86. **Smalheiser, N. R**. (2009) Do Neural Cells Communicate with Endothelial Cells via Secretory Exosomes and Microvesicles? Cardiovascular Psychiatry and Neurology, 2009: 383086.

87. **Smalheiser, N. R.,** Lugli, G., Lenon, A. L. Davis, J. M., Torvik, V. I. and Larson, J. R. (2010) Olfactory discrimination training up-regulates and reorganizes

expression of microRNAs in adult mouse hippocampus. ASN Neuro 2(1):art:e00028.

88. Cohen, A.M., Adams, C.E., Davis, J.M., Yu, C., Yu, P.S., Meng, W., Duggan, L., McDonagh, M., and **Smalheiser, N.R.** (2010). Evidence-based medicine, the changing landscape of the medical knowledge base, and the need for automated text mining tools. ACM 1st Intl. Conference on Health Informatics 1:376-380.

89. **Smalheiser, N. R.**, Lugli, G., Rizavi, H., Torvik, V. I., Turecki, G. and Dwivedi, Y.(2012) MicroRNA Expression is Down-Regulated and Reorganized in Prefrontal Cortex of Depressed Suicide. PLoS ONE 7: e33201.

90. **Smalheiser, N. R.**, Lugli, G., Thimmapuram, J., Cook, E. H. and Larson, J. (2011) Endogenous siRNAs and noncoding RNA-derived small RNAs are expressed in adult mouse hippocampus and are up-regulated in olfactory discrimination training. RNA 17: 166-181.

91. **Smalheiser, N.R.**, Lugli G., Zhang, H., Rizavi, H. S., Torvik, V.I., Pandey, G.N., Davis, J. M. and Dwivedi, Y. (2010) microRNA expression in rat brain exposed to repeated inescapable shock: differential alterations in learned helplessness vs. non-learned helplessness. Int. J. Neuropsychopharmacol. 14: 1315-1325.

92. **Smalheiser, N.R.**, Zhou, W. and Torvik, V.I. (2011) Distribution of "characteristic" terms in MEDLINE literatures. Information, *2*(2), 266-276.

93. **Smalheiser, N.R.** (2011). Sometimes non-IRB approved research deserves a second look. J. Clinical Research and Bioethics 2:104.

94. Piriyapongsa, J., Jordan, I.K., Conley, A. B., Tom Ronan and **Smalheiser, N.R.** (2010) Transcription factor binding sites are highly enriched within microRNA precursor sequences. Biology Direct 6: 61.

95. **Smalheiser, N. R.** (2011) Literature-based discovery: beyond the ABCs. J. Am. Information Sci. Technol. 63: 218-224.

96. **Smalheiser, N. R.**, Lugli, G., Thimmapuram, J., Cook, E. H. and Larson, J. (2011) Mitochondrial small RNAs that are up-regulated during olfactory discrimination training in mice. Mitochondrion 11: 994-995. doi:10.1016/j.mito.2011.08.014

97. **Smalheiser, N. R.** (2012). The search for endogenous siRNAs in the mammalian brain. Exp. Neurol 235: 455-463.

98. Lugli, G., Larson, J., Demars, M.P. and **Smalheiser, N. R.** (2012) Primary microRNA precursor transcripts are localized at postsynaptic densities in adult mouse forebrain. J. Neurochem 123: 459-466. Recommended by Faculty of 1000.

99. Shu, L., Lin, C., Meng, W., Han, Y., Yu, C. T., Smalheiser, N. R. (2012) A framework for entity

resolution with efficient blocking. 13th Intl. Conference on Information Reuse and Integration (IRI), pp.431-440.

100. **Smalheiser, N. R.** (2013) How many scientists does it take to change a paradigm? EMBO Reports 14: 861-865. doi:10.1038/embor.2013.125.

101. Shao, W., Adams, C.E., Cohen, A.M., Davis, J.M., McDonagh, M.S., Yu, P.S. and **Smalheiser, N. R.** (2014) Aggregator: A machine learning approach to identifying MEDLINE articles that derive from the same underlying clinical trial. Methods 74:65-70.

102. **Smalheiser, N.R.,** Lin, C., Jia, L., Jiang, Y., Cohen, A.M., Yu, C., Davis, J.M., Adams, C.E., McDonagh, M.S., and Meng, W. (2014) Design and implementation of Metta, a metasearch engine for biomedical literature intended for systematic reviewers. Health Information Science and Systems 2: 1.

103. Jiang, Y., Lin, C., Meng, W., Yu, C. and **Smalheiser, N.R.** (2014) Rule-based deduplication of article records across bibliographic databases. Database doi: 10.1093/database/bat086.

104. **Smalheiser, N.R.,** Lugli, G., Zhang, H., Rizavi, H., Cook, E.H. and Dwivedi, Y. (2014) Expression of microRNAs and other small RNAs in Prefrontal Cortex in Schizophrenia, Bipolar Disorder and Depressed Subjects. PLoS ONE 9: e86469. PMC3903529. Selected to be included in the PLOS ONE Human Genetics Editor's Picks Collection.

105. **Smalheiser, N.R.**, Zhang, H. and Dwivedi, Y. (2014) Enoxacin elevates miRNA expression in frontal cortex and prevents learned helplessness in rats. Frontiers in Psychiatry 5: 6. PMC3918929 Selected as being in the top 10% of articles in the journal and invited for a Tier 2 follow up article.

106. **Smalheiser, N. R.** (2014) The RNA-centered view of the synapse: noncoding RNAs and synaptic plasticity. Phil. Trans. Roy. Soc. B. 369: pii: 20130504.

107. Cohen, A.M., **Smalheiser, N.R.**, McDonagh, M.S., Yu, C., Adams, C.E., Davis, J.M., and Yu, P.S. (2015) Automated confidence ranked classification of randomized controlled trial articles: An aid to evidence-based medicine. JAMIA 22(3):707-17.

108. **Smalheiser, N. R.** and Gomes, O. L. A. (2014) Eukaryotic Argonaute-DNA binding? Biology Direct 10:27.

109. D'Souza, J.L. and **Smalheiser, N.R.** (2014) Three journal metrics and their application to biomedical journals. PLoS ONE 9(12): e115681.

110. **Smalheiser, N. R.**, Shao, W., and Yu, P. S. (2015) Nuggets: Findings shared in multiple clinical case reports. J. Med. Library Assoc. 103: 171-176.

111. De Groote, S. L., Schulz, M., and Smalheiser, N. R. (2015) Examining the impact of the National Institutes

of Health Public Access Policy on the citation rates of journal articles. PLoS ONE 10(10): e0139951. Won the 2016 Ida and George Eliot Prize of the Medical Library Association.

112. Lugli, G., Cohen, A.M., Bennett, D.A., Shah, R.C., Fields, C. J., Hernandez, A. G., and **Smalheiser, N. R.** (2015) Plasma Exosomal miRNAs in persons with and without Alzheimer Disease: Altered expression and prospects for biomarkers. PLoS ONE 10 (10): e0139233.

113. Dwivedi Y, Roy B, Lugli G, Rizavi H, Zhang H, and Smalheiser NR. (2015) Chronic corticosterone-mediated dysregulation of microRNA network in prefrontal cortex of rats: relevance to depression pathophysiology. Transl Psychiatry 5: e682.

114. **Smalheiser, N. R.** and Bonifield, G. (2016) Two Similarity Metrics for Medical Subject Headings (MeSH): An Aid to Biomedical Text Mining and Author Name Disambiguation. J. Biomed. Discovery Collab. 7: e1.

115. Kehoe, A., Torvik, V., Ross, M. and Smalheiser, N. Predicting MeSH beyond MEDLINE. Workshop on Scholarly Web Mining '17 February 10, 2017, Cambridge, UK. DOI 10.1145/3057148.3057155.

116. Peng, Y., Bonifield, G. and **Smalheiser, N. R.** (2017)Gaps within Biomedical Literatures: Strategies for

Discovery. Frontiers in Research Metrics & Analytics, 22 May 2017 | https://doi.org/10.3389/frma.2017.00003.

117. **Byron C. Wallace**, Anna Noel-Storr, Iain J Marshall, Aaron M. Cohen, Neil R. Smalheiser and James Thomas. (2017) Identifying Reports of Randomized Controlled Trials (RCTs) via a Hybrid Machine Learning and Crowdsourcing Approach. Journal of the American Medical Informatics Association. 2017 May 25, https://doi.org/10.1093/jamia/ocx053.

118. **Smalheiser, N. R.** (2017) Rediscovering Don Swanson: The past, present and future of literature based discovery. J. Data Information Sci., 2 (4): 43-64. doi: 10.1515/jdis-2017-0019.

119. **Smalheiser, N. R.** and Cohen, A. M. (2018) Design of a generic, open platform for machine learning-assisted indexing and clustering of articles in PubMed, a biomedical bibliographic database. Data and Information Management 2: 21-36. https://doi.org/10.2478/dim-2018-0004.

120. **Cohen, A.M.**, Dunivin, Z. and Smalheiser, N.R. (2018) A Probabilistic Automated Tagger to Identify Human-Related Publications. Database 2018: 1-8. https://doi.org/10.1093/database/bay079

121. **Cohen, A.M.** and Smalheiser, N. R. (2018) UIC/OHSU CLEF 2018 Task 2 Diagnostic Test Accuracy Ranking using Publication Type Cluster

Similarity Measures. CLEF 2018 Working Notes: Working Notes of CLEF 2018 - Conference and Labs of the Evaluation Forum, in press. Ed. Linda Cappellato, Nicola Ferro, Jian-Yun Nie, Laure Soulier, CEUR-WS Proceedings, n. 2125.

122. **Smalheiser NR,** Cohen AM, Bonifield G. Unsupervised low-dimensional vector representations for words, phrases and text that are transparent, scalable, and produce similarity metrics that are not redundant with neural embeddings. J Biomed Inform. 2019 Feb;90:103096. doi: 10.1016/j.jbi.2019.103096. Epub 2019 Jan 14.

123. **Smalheiser, N. R.,** Luo, M., Addepalli, S., and Cui, X. (2019) A Manual Corpus of Annotated Main Findings of Clinical Case Reports. Database 2019: 2019, bay143. doi: 10.1093/database/bay143.

124. **Smalheiser, N. R.** (2019) Mining Clinical Case Reports to Identify New Lines of Investigation in Alzheimer Disease: the Curious Case of DNase I. Journal of Alzheimer's Disease Reports 3 (1): 71-76.

125. **Smalheiser NR.** Ketamine: A Neglected Therapy for Alzheimer Disease. Front Aging Neurosci. 2019 Jul 24;11:186. doi: 10.3389/fnagi.2019.00186.

126. **Smalheiser NR.** A Neglected Link Between the Psychoactive Effects of Dietary Ingredients and Consciousness-Altering Drugs. Front Psychiatry. 2019 Aug 16;10:591. doi: 10.3389/fpsyt.2019.00591.

127. **Smalheiser NR**, Holt AW. New improved Aggregator: predicting which clinical trial articles derive from the same registered clinical trial. JAMIA Open. 2020 Oct 28;3(3):338-341. doi: 10.1093/jamiaopen/ooaa042.

128. Linh Hoang; Yogeshwar Kansara; Neil R. Smalheiser; Aaron M. Cohen; **Jodi Schneider**. (2019) Evaluation of an automated probabilistic RCT Tagger applied to published Cochrane reviews. Jamia Open, in press.

129. **Smalheiser NR**, Fragnito DP, Tirk EE. Anne O'Tate: Value-added PubMed search engine for analysis and text mining. PLoS One. 2021 Mar 8;16(3):e0248335. doi: 10.1371/journal.pone.0248335.

130. **Neil R Smalheiser**, Jodi Schneider, Vetle I Torvik, Dean P Fragnito, Eric E Tirk. The Citation Cloud of a Biomedical Article: Enabling Citation Analysis. MedRxiv **doi:** https://doi.org/10.1101/2020.06.15.20131623, also submitted to J Med Library Assoc.

131. **Smalheiser NR**, Graetz EE, Yu Z, Wang J. Effect size, sample size and power of forced swim test assays in mice: Guidelines for investigators to optimize reproducibility. PLoS One. 2021 Feb 24;16(2):e0243668. doi: 10.1371/journal.pone.0243668.

INVITED BOOK CHAPTERS

Smalheiser, N. R. (2005) The Arrowsmith project: 2005 status report. Discovery Science 2005. Lecture Notes in Artificial Intelligence vol. 3735, eds. A. Hoffmann, H. Motoda, and T. Scheffer, pp. 26-43, Springer-Verlag Press, Berlin. (Invited lecture at the 8th International Conference on Discovery Science / 16th International Conference on Algorithmic Learning Theory (Singapore, October 2005), published as a book chapter.)

Smalheiser, N.R. and Torvik, V. I. (2006) Complications in mammalian microRNA target prediction. In "MicroRNA: Protocols", ed. S.-Y. Ying, in the series "Methods in Molecular Biology', published by Humana Press, pp. 115-127.

Smalheiser, N. R. and Torvik, V. I. (2008) Models of microRNA-target coordination. In "microRNAs: From Basic Science to Disease Biology", ed. K. Appasani, Cambridge University Press, pp. 221-226.

Smalheiser, N. R. and Torvik, V. I. (2008). The place of literature based discovery in contemporary scientific practice. In "Literature-Based Discovery", ed. P. Bruza and M. Weeber, Springer Press, pp. 13-22.

Lugli, G. and **Smalheiser, N. R.** (2013). Preparing Synaptoneurosomes from Adult Mouse Forebrain. In MicroRNA: Protocols, part of the series Methods in Molecular Biology published by Humana Press. 936: 173-179.

BOOKS AND JOURNAL SPECIAL ISSUES
AUTHORED, EDITED OR CO-EDITED
Tiffany C. Veinot, Ümit V. Çatalyürek, Gang
Luo, Henrique Andrade, Neil R. Smalheiser (Eds.):
ACM International Health Informatics Symposium, IHI
2010, Arlington, VA, USA, November 11 - 12, 2010,
Proceedings. ACM 2010, ISBN 978-1-4503-0030-8.

Andrade, H. and Smalheiser, Neil R. (eds.): *Journal of Medical Systems* special issue, 2011.

Yanchun Zhang, Guiqing Yao, Jing He, Lei Wang, Neil
R. Smalheiser, Xiaoxia Yin (Eds.): Health Information
Science: Third International Conference, HIS 2014,
Shenzhen, China, April 22–23, 2014, Proceedings,
Lecture Notes in Computer Science 8423, Springer.

Smalheiser, N.R. and Cohen, A.M. Models of
Discovery: Mining the scientific literature. Special issue
for *Journal of Data and Information Science*, 2017.

Chen, C., Smalheiser, N. R. et al. editors: Frontiers
Research Topic: Science Mapping: Resources, Tools,
and Benchmarks, for *Frontiers in Research Metrics and Analytics*, 2017.

Lu, L., Smalheiser, N. R., et al. editors: Special issue on
Data Analysis, Information Organization, and
Knowledge Discovery in Smart Health for *Data and Information Management*, 2018.

Smalheiser, N. R. Data Literacy: How to Make your Experiments Robust and Reproducible. Academic Press, in production, 2017. Textbook intended mainly for graduate students in the sciences; I am sole author.

Special issues of Frontiers in Scholarly Metrics and Analytics, two subjects : LBD and Covid, 2021.

SCIENTIFIC CORRESPONDENCE, EDITORIALS AND BOOK REVIEWS
Smalheiser, N. and Philipson, L.(1984) Alternative medicine. New Engl J Med 310: 791.
Smalheiser, N. (1984) More on the Medical College Admission Test. New Engl J Med 311(12): 803.
Smalheiser, N. (1988) Means to immortalize neural cells. Trends in Neurosci. 11: 307.
Smalheiser, N. R. (1990) Young scientists and the future. Science 249: 1486-1487.
Smalheiser, N. R. (1992) Teaching the Human Genome Project as a case study. J. College Science Teaching. 22: 7.
Smalheiser, N. R. (1994) review of Evolution without Selection: Form and Function by Autoevolution. Perspect. Biol. Med. 37: 312-313.
Smalheiser, N. R., De Groote, S. L. and Case, M. M. (2009) Open-access publishing: a new path. J. Biomed. Discovery Collaboration 4: 6.

JOURNAL COVERS
Cell Adhesion & Communication 5: (6), 1998.
Cerebral Cortex 9: (8), 1999.

PUBLIC WEB-DEPOSITED DATABASES

Smalheiser, N.R. and Torvik, V.I. (2004) A statistical approach predicts human microRNA targets. Genome Biol. 5: P4. http://genomebiology.com/2004/5/2/P4.

Zhou, W., Torvik, V. I. and **Smalheiser, N. R.** (2007) A database of terms in MEDLINE abstracts that co-occur frequently and share the same semantic category. Deposited on the Arrowsmith website.

D'Souza, J.L. and **Smalheiser, N.R.** (2014) Three journal metrics and their application to biomedical journals. Data posted at http://arrowsmith.psych.uic.edu/arrowsmith_uic/journal_metrics.html.

Smalheiser, N. R. and Bonifield, G. (2016) Two Similarity Metrics for Medical Subject Headings (MeSH): An Aid to Biomedical Text Mining and Author Name Disambiguation. Data posted at http://arrowsmith.psych.uic.edu/arrowsmith_uic/mesh_pair_metrics.html.

Smalheiser, N. R. and Bonifield, G. (2018) Term and Text Similarity Metrics. Data posted at http://arrowsmith.psych.uic.edu/arrowsmith_uic/word_similarity_metrics.html.

PROJECT-RELATED PUBLICATIONS (supervised but was not a co-author)

Zhou, W. and Yu, C. (2005) Experiment report of TREC 2005 Genomics track ad hoc retrieval task. *The Fourteenth Text REtrieval Conference (TREC 2005) Proceedings*, Baltimore, MD. Technical report, http://ir.ohsu.edu/genomics/.

Swanson, D. R. (2006) Atrial fibrillation in athletes: Implicit literature-based connections suggest that overtraining and subsequent inflammation may be a contributory mechanism. Med. Hypotheses 66: 1085-1092.

Swanson, D. R. (2008) Running, esophageal acid reflux, and atrial fibrillation: a chain of events linked by evidence from separate medical literatures. Med. Hypotheses 71: 178-185.

Swanson, D. R. (2011) Literature-based resurrection of neglected medical discoveries. J. Biomed. Discovery Collab 6: 34-47.

TECHICAL REPORTS (not peer-reviewed)
Zhou, W., Yu, C., Torvik, V. I. and Smalheiser, N. R. (2006) A concept-based framework for passage retrieval in Genomics. *Fifteenth Text REtrieval Conference (TREC 2006) Proceedings*, Baltimore, WA.

Torvik, V. I., Smalheiser, N. R. and Weeber, M. (2007) A simple Perl tokenizer and stemmer for biomedical text. Posted on the Arrowsmith website to accompany the Biomedical Stemmer and Tokenizer tool.

Smalheiser, N. R. and Lugli, G. (2014) Preparation of synaptosomes from postmortem human brain. bioRxiv (preprint repository). doi: http://dx.doi.org/10.1101/006510.

Smalheiser, N. R. and Bonifield, G. (2016) Two Similarity Metrics for Medical Subject Headings (MeSH): An Aid to Biomedical Text Mining and Author Name Disambiguation. bioRxiv (preprint repository). doi: http://dx.doi.org/10.1101/039008

Smalheiser, N. R. and Bonifield, G. (2018) Unsupervised Low-Dimensional Vector Representations for Words, Phrases and Text that are Transparent, Scalable, and produce Similarity Metrics that are Complementary to Neural Embeddings. arXiv (preprint repository) https://arxiv.org/abs/1801.01884.

www.ingramcontent.com/pod-product-compliance
Lightning Source LLC
La Vergne TN
LVHW051629080426
835511LV00016B/2254